D1478456

Fifty-Fifty

The Clarity of Hindsight

Julie L. Kessler

Strategic Book Publishing and Rights Co.

Strategic Book Publishing and Rights Co.
12620 FM 1960, Suite A4-507
Houston, TX 77065
www.sbpra.com

ISBN: 978-1-62212-218-9

To my mother, daughter, and husband: my personal trifecta of having been given life, having given birth, and having given and received an abundance of love. You are my raison d'être and my air, for the last fifty years and the next fifty. And to my dear Burt, the very best friend ever in the history of the world. For yesterday, for today and for tomorrow.

With love always, JLK

Foreword

When I sat down in the departure lounge of Air Asia at Changi Airport in Singapore and started tapping away at my laptop as I waited for my flight to Denpasar, I could hardly believe the title I had typed. Who in the hell was *fifty* years old and what did I have to say about that anyway?

The harsh reality is that despite continuous exercise and reading to stay fit in both body and mind, attempted sun avoidance to postpone the losing wrinkle battle, and my fifty-year-old husband's description of me as his much younger wife, I was in fact staring head on at the big five-oh. Although I couldn't quite believe it myself, on that day in July in Singapore, and contrary to my kind husband's assertions, I was, in fact, fifty years old.

But what did I have to say about that which would be worth reading? I'm still not sure, but hope that readers will indulge me while I recount some of the more important lessons I've learned along this fascinating and well-traveled road.

A friend I have known for more than twenty years, who is forty-nine and who also happens to be my dentist, told me a couple of weeks ago, while staring into my mouth, that the thing that freaked him out the most about turning fifty was not the actual number, but "the idea that his ride was more than half-way over." While I certainly understood what he was talking about, I don't think of it that way at all. This is mostly because I think the second half of life is so much more interesting than the first half in the sense that we are more aware of who we are and much more accepting of the person we have become. We are also much more aware of what's important in life, and also more aware that, just like a roll of paper towels, life goes much faster as you near the end. Or perhaps as you inch closer to the next journey onward.

As a child and teenager, I used to ask my mother what age she wished she could be. She would always respond in the same way. She wanted to be exactly the age she was at that moment, but perhaps with the body of a younger woman. She was very clear that she didn't want to be eighteen or twenty-one again, or even thirty. She appreciated the insight and wisdom that living gave her, and accepted with a rare grace the often bizarre road she traveled right up to the end of her life, which came just three months following her fifty-first birthday.

In her honor, and to mid-centurions everywhere, I devote these writings. The very best is right now and exactly where you are headed. Wherever that may be.

JLK

Table of Contents

Fifty-Fifty

The Clarity of Hindsight

1

Travel a lot. Pack lightly.

Everyone who knows me, even marginally, knows I love to travel. Some of my friends call me by the honorific Jet Fuel Jules. It is a moniker I've worn proudly. Indeed, there was a period when I could recite from memory airfares to certain cities abroad and seat configurations of many aircraft. And I knew all about the latest and best gravity-defying carry-on wheelie bags. I still travel a lot, but it has become more mindful now that I have a husband, career, kids, dogs, and a house. I've come to believe, however, that all those responsibilities of life and the desire to travel the world are, as Tim Cahill so aptly put it in the *Accidental Explorer's Guide to Patagonia*, "not necessarily antagonistic ambitions."

There are so many amazing places the world over that can airmail the soul into overdrive. There is an openness and a vulnerability when one travels in unfamiliar locales. It creates a certain ability to step outside yourself. While trying the new and the different, one actually gets to *be* new and different almost effortlessly, and without the confining judgments usually encountered on home turf. That is why travel so often alters you after the fact. Even when you're back in the routine of life. Often in immeasurable ways, and more often than not, for the better.

I've noticed, though, that two people can go to the same destination, even at the same time, and have such different experiences. I believe that this is because how we view the world and our place in it is filtered through the prism of our past. Along with whatever baggage we possess which won't, no matter how hard we try, fit into the overhead compartment. It is also filtered by whatever we need to learn at the time. Sometimes we're open to the lesson right before our eyes, and sometimes we're not. Books can certainly transport us to another world and another time, but travel on the other hand, can often transport you to an altogether different state of being.

As Mark Jenkins correctly wrote in *The Ghost Road,*

> Adventure is a path. Real adventure—self-determined, self-motivated, often risky—forces you to have firsthand encounters with the world. The world the way it is, not the way you imagine it. Your body will collide with the earth and you will bear witness. In this way, you will be compelled to grapple with the limitless kindness and bottomless cruelty of humankind—and perhaps realize that you yourself are capable of both. This will change you. Nothing will ever again be black-and-white.

Personally, I have never gone for hard-core adventure travel—not for a lack of interest, but probably out of simple self-preservation. The most "adventurous" thing I've ever done was probably a twelve-hour trek starting a few miles outside the small mountain resort town of Sapa, about 400 miles north of Hanoi, near the Chinese border, in the company of an interpreter and eight women from the traditional Red Dao tribe. These women ranged in age from twenty-five to forty. And the reason I know this is because these women's response to the presence of a Caucasian woman in their remote area of the world went in one swift breath, something like this: "Hi, and how old ARE you?" Thus, to be polite, as I learned from my interpreter, I was obliged to ask the same question in return. It was an interesting and glorious outing with its fair share of craggy, narrow, and often wet and frightening invisible mountain trails to traverse in order to reach the women's remote mountain village, which was spread across the mountain top. But the trip was worth it, notwithstanding the recurring shakiness in my legs—though I made it a point never, ever to look down. Besides their colorful and very thick traditional layered clothing, they each wore what appeared to be five pounds of ornate silver jewelry. Even though I had an inkling that I was certainly not in Kansas anymore, I was not prepared mentally for the extremely harsh nature of this tribe's existence, which I'm pretty sure has not changed in the last several hundred years. Water was still pumped by hand from outdoor spigots, none of the thatched huts had electricity, grain was stored in loft-like structures above their sleeping areas, oxen did hard field labor, and chickens and goats roamed freely underfoot. And I'm fairly certain none of these women (who all looked decades older than their stated ages) or their children had ever seen a medical school trained doctor. I had been told to bring small, lightweight gifts for the village children we would encounter along the way, and so I was armed with a cache of lollipops, ballpoint pens and balloons. It became clear that these children had never seen a balloon before and didn't know their purpose. Much to my horror, several had put them right into their mouths and started chewing them, believing them to be some oddball western candy, until the interpreter showed them how to blow them up.

I also once went on a shark-feeding scuba dive in French Polynesia with a PADI-certified dive master who was clearly fearless, or perhaps just senseless. We had gone down to about sixty feet below the surface with a large, party-sized, plastic Igloo-style ice chest secured by a rope tethered to our boat overhead. When the group of six divers and the dive master had equalized our pressure and weights so that we would be still at the bottom of the ocean floor, the dive master tugged on the rope tied to the chest. Then the captain, who remained on-board the boat, pulled on the rope until it and the ice chest's lid disappeared. Inside the ice chest, which we really hoped contained cold beer, were instead perhaps fifty pounds of freshly dead and bloody fish. In a matter of maybe five seconds, there were at least thirty sharks, many of which were six or seven feet in length, circling the group in what can only be described as a total feeding frenzy. There were black-tip sharks, lemon sharks and a few hammerhead sharks, which we were told weren't interested in eating mere mortals when there was fresh, lifeless fish to be had. This is all well and good on a theoretical level, but every certified diver knows that sharks are virtually blind, and I surely didn't want to be confused for a Cro-Magnon culinary delight. Shark skin is also like very harsh sand paper and I didn't want any of them bumping into me either. In a tribute to what can only be described as good genes and perhaps even better luck, it was nothing short of a major miracle that I didn't have a myocardial infarction right then and there. That I lived to tell this story only proves just how blind sharks really are. All I could think of that evening, following several martinis—beer simply would not have had the requisite speedy medicinal effect—was that this particular dive was by far the stupidest thing I had done to date. And trust me, I have done some pretty damned stupid things in fifty years.

There have also been the more "usual" scary travel experiences. I had my purse torn off my shoulder one summer evening by two young punks whizzing by on a motor scooter on a street in Seville, Spain. And I was once closely followed by an older Arab man in a narrow and winding part of the old Kasbah in Tangier, Morocco, who made disparaging comments about my alleged ethnicity. I finally turned around to face the old man and stared him down in a lame attempt not to show any fear. But I was scared. The old Arab was correct in his ethnic allegations—not that I came clean to him as to my bloodlines, since I did not wish to leave any of mine there on the street as a Moroccan souvenir. These isolated negative experiences notwithstanding, I can say with certainty that, while unpleasant at best, they would not stop me and have not stopped me from continuing my travels.

I've often said that traveling abroad made me more American. More American in the sense that, while abroad, I've often felt like some sort of ambassador, and, oddly, found myself defending presidents I didn't vote for and policies I abhorred. This was most certainly the case during my travels while George W. inhabited the White House. It was a bizarre juxtaposition that I haven't always been able to explain, even to myself. Somehow, being abroad, or if you are lucky, living abroad as an expatriate, allows a certain larger ability to be American. And then when I would return home, I'd find that I would put on my international hat, arguing the position or policy of whatever country I had just come from.

Travel also allows one, it seems, to be American in a way one simply cannot while stateside. I have found that I am somehow able to see myself in purely national terms, allowing me to dismiss race, religion, locale and even family while on the road. Traveling for an extended period of time or being an expatriate permits a certain illusion, allowing the traveler to try on different ways of identifying as an American in its most theoretical form. Or perhaps it allows a level of understanding, self-invention or reinvention of which one is deprived at home.

Also important is the fact that changes of scenery often serve to remind you of other possibilities and other avenues in your own life. It is not always necessary to hop on an aluminum tin can and head into the sometimes-turbulent skies at 30,000 feet in order to do that. However, a physical change of scenery often gives you a psychological perspective that may simply be unattainable in the familiar surroundings of your home turf. And it is okay to feel lost sometimes and go in search of finding your way, with or without a good map. Sometimes getting lost helps you get found. But when you go, and go you should, wherever you think might tickle your fancy or pique your interest, pack as lightly as possible. Figuratively and literally. Make sure and leave all of your preconceived notions and expectations at home. If you want everything and everyone to be exactly the same as at home, then there is little point in making the journey. The whole point is to see differently, go differently, be different and learn from all that those differences entail. And as a practical matter, nearly everything you think you might need (but probably don't) can be bought wherever you are headed. So pack lightly. You—and your back, neck and shoulders—will be glad you did.

2

You are your own harshest critic. I promise.

The sad fact is that, in general, no one will beat you up to the extent and degree that you yourself will and often do. Sometimes I will hear someone—and that someone is often me—say something awful, outrageous, or simply out-of-whack with the circumstances, and think, *Mamma mia*, I would never let *someone else* speak to me that way, so why on earth do I let *myself* speak to me that way? If you can't pose the question to yourself in this manner, imagine that you are talking to your closest friend or your daughter about the issue in question. I bet you would be far kinder.

While men can often criticize and beat themselves up with the best of them, it is no secret that women are often their own harshest and worst critics. This sort of negative self-judgment often leads directly—in fact, it's a one-way ticket—to feelings of guilt. We often believe we fail as women if we don't hit a homerun in every inning or succeed in every avenue of our lives – and look damned good at the same time. Whoever said, "You can have it all!" should be shot on sight. We can ask her precisely what she meant by that following the shooting. This concept sets women up for continuous feelings of failure if that homerun, or several in fact, aren't hit in every single inning while they are doing seventy-six other things well at exactly the same time. I prefer instead the idea that you *can* have it all, but that you cannot have it all *at the same time*.

For three years prior to the arrival of our daughter, I was in-house counsel to a busy outpatient surgical facility. I worked full-time and the hours were fairly controllable. But often I had to work more than full-time. In fact, on the day my daughter was born, I worked right up until my husband picked me up and drove me to the hospital to give birth. Three weeks later, I returned to work.

The problem was that while I was at work, all I wanted to do was get home and be with my daughter. This led to an almost irrational jealousy of our kind-hearted babysitter. And while I was at home, all I could think about were my professional responsibilities and the mountain of work piling up. My anxiety levels rose while I prayed for five hours of uninterrupted sleep so that my brain could function at the level necessary to do a good job at work. As I compiled monumental to-do lists in my sleep-deprived brain, I simultaneously wondered how it was humanly possible that an organism which weighed less than the average French poodle could possibly soil diapers as fast as I could change them. I was nearly terminally exhausted and felt that I was unable to do both things well at the same time and in the way I thought I needed and wanted to. I was left with feelings of guilt in every arena of my life, hearing in my sleep-deprived state that deceptive mantra that "You can have it all"—all the while feeling that somehow I simply wasn't working hard enough or doing enough, despite the constant fatigue. After a few months, I figured out that the mantra was a bloody lie, as I knew I was doing my best—but something simply had to change.

So I started to work part-time. Though as most part-time professionals know, a part-time position is never truly a part-time job. It is something more like a three-quarter time job at part-time pay. It was probably a reincarnation of one of those "new math" questions I never really understood the first time around. But never mind; money wasn't really the burning issue at the time. Working part-time allowed me to feel as though I was then truly doing my very best, both as a professional and as a mother. It was a good balance, and the guilt-inducing angst started to fade. When I was at the office, I was focused and glad to be there, and to stay connected with my professional needs and obligations. At home, my jealousy of the babysitter turned into unmitigated gratitude. And what sleep I did get was more restful. I never did, however, figure out that French poodle thing. Perhaps you have to be born on French soil to figure that one out.

"Good" guilt is your own personal Jiminy Cricket. Your internal Jiminy gives you the ability to tell right from wrong in your life. The other type of guilt, Jiminy's evil and dastardly neighbor, the one always throwing trash on your side of the property line, is the toxic one. Toxic guilt is the good Jiminy on an overdose of anabolic steroids. This is not gratuitous chest-beating. Toxic guilt often leads to high levels of angst and then, if the situation causing the guilt is left unchanged, it can turn into depression. Sometimes it's just a matter of perspective, requiring that you stand back for a bit. If a respected friend were in the same position, would you judge him or her as harshly as you are judging yourself? The answer is almost universally no.

Sometimes, though, you need to lower your expectations. Or modify those one-size-fits-all concepts which are catchy in theory and sell lots of copy, but are unrealistic for many when put into practice. I am not saying to sell out what is important to you, but adjust yourself to the current reality. Lowering your expectations or modifying the status quo to fit your needs and your situation means that a welcome dissipation of angst is often the outcome. I am not in any way suggesting that by lowering your expectations you shouldn't do your best in whatever endeavor or arena you are involved in; on the contrary, your internal Jiminy requires precisely that you do your very best. But that is really all that we mere mortals can, in fact, do. If you truly believe that you are doing your level best, then, by definition, that must be enough. And that is the case even if the results aren't exactly—or even remotely—what you would like them to be. Or if, indeed, you end up somewhere altogether different. The acknowledgement of your humanity is all that is required in order to start hushing that harsh critic within. Check out the mirror; you will find there a very human reflection. Then hush you must.

3

Sometimes the best-laid plans to travel to exotic places end up taking you home, though to an entirely different place from the one you left.

It was mid-1983 and I had just graduated from university. My Israeli born half- brother and I had been making plans for several months and saving every nickel along the way so that we could take a year off and travel the world. This, we thought, would give us a chance to get to know each other better. We also hoped that it might make up, at least partially anyway, for the complete dearth of any shared childhood memories. We researched various modes of transportation and plotted a map, then researched some more. We talked to several people who had done the "year off" and got many pearls of wisdom. Often the most important of those was where to avoid. We finally decided that since we would be gone so long, we had to have a car, and we figured if we ever really got stuck somewhere, we could always sleep in it for a night. More research ensued, and we ended up buying a small black Volkswagen at the duty-free shop at Schipol Airport in Amsterdam, Holland. In those days you could buy chocolates, perfumes, vodka and yes, automobiles. I remember thinking at the time that buying a car at an airport was by far the coolest thing ever.

We spent about a week in Holland visiting a medical school buddy of my half-brother's, then an artist acquaintance of mine whom I had met through a friend in the U.S. We drove through Belgium, then on to Germany, where we stayed about a month with friends and where I taught aerobics classes at a gym in Cologne to Donna Summer's music, which was then all the rage in Germany. We then left, headed through Austria and on to what was then Yugoslavia for nearly a month, where we drove along the Adriatic coast, stopping in small villages and seaside towns. It was both beautiful and interesting, though I clearly remember having to stand in line in the mornings to buy a loaf of bread and being shocked to enter small supermarkets and see completely empty shelves. It was also the place where I drank some bad fruit juice purchased at one of those nearly-barren-shelved markets and was the sickest I had ever been in my life. I simply couldn't move. Ten days later, and ten pounds lighter on my part, we drove on to Greece. After a couple of weeks there, taking in the historic sights and seeing some of the gorgeous islands, we made plans to go on to Israel.

So we bought tickets for a ship departing from Piraeus. The day of departure came and we drove the little black VW into the bowels of the enormous boat, then took our seats a few decks above. The ship was packed to capacity and seemingly beyond that. Since we had very little money, we bought the cheapest seats possible. I remember there being only a couple of restrooms for about 200 people on our deck. Considering it took three days to get to Israel, we only used the restrooms when we became desperate. The ship stopped for an afternoon on the beautiful island of Crete and then for a day on the troubled Mediterranean island of Cyprus. Finally we arrived in Israel, where I was to meet some of my half-brother's extended family, including his other half-siblings from his father's second marriage, as well as meet some of my own distant relatives for the first time. We were in Israel not two days when our long-planned one year international adventure came abruptly and painfully to a screeching halt. I learned by telephone that the mother we shared was sick with terminal cancer in a hospital in Hawaii. The beginning, middle and end of her tragic illness and death came in fewer than three obscenely short months.

Trying to return to the U.S. immediately from Tel-Aviv during the busy summer season was unbelievably hard. I couldn't get a seat out at any price for over two weeks. In a panic I called everyone I knew there, no matter how remote. Finally, an uncle who had just arrived back to Tel-Aviv from a business trip to South Africa and who worked pretty high up in the national carrier, El-Al, intervened and got me a seat to New York through London. I got to Ben-Gurion Airport the next day and was promptly denied exit since I had arrived by ship in the northern port city of Haifa two days earlier with the little diesel-engine VW. In those days and perhaps still today, only tourists and cab drivers were permitted to have diesel-engine cars in Israel. So the car had to leave with me in order for me to exit the country, regardless of the personal circumstances with which I was confronted. I tried everything I could think of that day, even offering a bond for the full price of the car to assure I would return at some point to retrieve it and remove it from the country. But no amount of hysterical crying, or cajoling in any language, helped.

Furious and freaked out given how hard it had been to get an airline seat in the first place, I left the airport and hailed a cab out of Ben-Gurion. I called the uncle who had helped me with the ticket and told him what had happened at immigration and then returned to the home of a distant cousin where the VW was parked. I left my bags at her home and then drove two hours north back to Haifa where I had just arrived a couple of days before. I had to find a cargo ship departing soon, for anywhere outside of Israel where the VW could sit until I could deal with it. The first shipping company I went to had a boat leaving for North Africa the next day which had room for the car, but I decided to try a few other companies, hoping against hope I might find a ship going closer to where I was headed. My third attempt found me at the offices of Zim Shipping Lines; they had a ship leaving for Long Beach, in Southern California, in three days. They had space for the car and I paid the exorbitant last-minute passage rate of $2,000, which left me with about fifty dollars to my name. Armed with a thick wad of bills of lading and vehicle exit papers, I called my uncle in the hope he could do his magic once again and get me a seat out in three days. He did, getting me a seat to New York through Athens and Rome. Looking back, those few days were complete hell. And anyone who has ever had the great misfortune to have to deal with Israeli bureaucracy can certainly confirm this. It is mind-bogglingly difficult, inefficient, heated, high-pitched, smoke-filled and devoid of anything even remotely resembling logic. Those who complain incessantly about French bureaucracy (and complain they should, as it is truly awful) have never, ever, had to deal with the grinding and noisy wheels of the brain-numbing Israeli bureaucracy. Make no mistake, Israel is a country I love deeply and profoundly—a place which feels intimately familiar to me because of the language, culture and music, and yet simultaneously feels oddly foreign since I was born, raised and socialized an American. However, dealing with its bureaucracy made me want to do something I would never otherwise consider in any country, namely spit, in total, unmitigated disgust.

Armed with the requisite paperwork and the coveted airline seat, I returned to Ben-Gurion, passed the expected intense security, and then once again went to the departure line. I gave all of my papers to the immigration official. I was made to wait about half an hour while he determined that I had everything I needed to leave, and was finally allowed to pass and head on to the gate. In my frenzy to get home, it only dawned on me when the plane finally took off that this bloody ball and chain of four wheels and metal might be denied exit off of the ship when it arrived in Long Beach three weeks later since it was a European model. I, of course, didn't give a damn. I arrived in New York but couldn't secure a direct seat to Los Angeles to continue on to Hawaii. My flight from New York therefore stopped in Cincinnati, Chicago, Salt Lake City, Phoenix and finally, as if in another galaxy altogether, Los Angeles. I then caught a flight to

Honolulu, and finally, a commuter plane to Maui. By the time I arrived in Kahului two-and-a-half days after I left Tel-Aviv, I could hardly state my name with any degree of certainty.

It so happened that a neighbor of my mother's was working at the airport that day and was just getting off work when I arrived at the gate. He gave me a lift home, and I dropped off my bags at the house, got into my mother's car, and drove straight to the hospital. In her typical selfless manner—and to this day, when I ponder that afternoon, it still blows my mind—the first thing my mother said to me following a big hug and kiss was that she "was so very sorry she had ruined my trip." This was a woman who would relentlessly do whatever was needed for others without stopping for even a second to think about it, and she simply refused to be a burden on anyone, even as she lay dying.

On the table next to her bed was a large bouquet of long-stemmed roses. They were from a physician in that hospital's emergency room with whom she had worked for several years during her second career as a psychiatric nurse. This physician always wore cowboy boots, and had a foot-long braid which hung down the back of the cowboy hat he always donned outside the emergency room, and sometimes in it. He and my mother had shared the kind of kindred spiritual bond that two people with the most disparate backgrounds humanly possible can sometimes together possess. Over the ensuing weeks, it became clear to me that he loved my mother deeply in the way a young motherless nephew loves a favored older aunt. If ever there was an earthbound angel dressed up as a Hawaiian cowboy with a wrinkled, ill-fitting white coat, it was this man. He not only became my friend, but patiently and gently guided me through the medical morass that became every breath of my existence during that horrible period of my life. If a person needed an inspirational figure to emulate if one had any aspirations at all of becoming a physician, it was most definitely this man.

My mother remained in the hospital for another six weeks, and then, as there was little else they could do for her other than pain management, everyone agreed she could go home with me. My mother and I had three good weeks together, talking late into the night about the improbable journey on which life had taken her, her high hopes for me, and her concerns that because of the way life was turning out, I, her only American bred and born child, would now be left alone in the U.S. There was so much I didn't know, and we had so little time left together. But we grabbed and made the most out of every possible minute together. Even in those days filled with chemical-induced nausea, she never for a second lost her wicked and often absurd sense of humor. Those who knew my mother would readily admit that she had turned laughter and laughing into an abstract art form. She had already lost her hair from the effects of the failed chemotherapy, and would occasionally wear a wig when someone came over to the house. One afternoon a neighbor came by, bringing tropical fruit from her garden. When the neighbor left after the short visit, my mother exaggeratedly yanked her wig off, threw it across the living room and yelled out, "Watch out for the squirrel!" I reminded her that squirrels, at least Hawaiian squirrels, did not fly. We both cracked up laughing until we were short of breath.

I was only twenty-one years old at the time, and our roles had unceremoniously been reversed. I was now the caretaker and she, physically, the child. I remember one evening as I was helping her bathe, she said to me that her dying of cancer was and would be far harder on me than it ever was on her. With all of her suffering in those last few weeks, those words burned a hole into my already-breaking heart.

At the end of three weeks at home, she said she wanted to return to the hospital, intuitively knowing, I imagine, that the end was near. It was, I later realized, in a fashion typical of her character, an incredibly generous act on her part. Two days later she no longer recognized me. It took me a very long time to forgive the careless nursing staff then assigned to her, who knew both of us and whom I passed that morning at the nurse's station on the way to her room, for not warning me that the cancer had metastasized to her brain, rendering her unable to recognize anyone. I have never had a shock like that before or since, and I pray I never will again.

The next day, an old friend had stopped by the house where I had returned briefly to shower and insisted I have a quick bite to eat with him before returning to the hospital. I declined, but he insisted, and going was easier than talking about why I didn't want to go anywhere or be with anyone. Out of my normally anal-retentive character, I forgot to close and lock the front sliding glass door to the house, and got into his car. As he was pulling out of the driveway with Hawaiian slack-key guitar loudly playing on the radio, he told me he thought he heard my home phone ringing. How he could hear anything over the beautiful but very loud music can now only be described as a divine aural intervention. I got out of the car, walked up the long driveway, and, sure enough, the phone was ringing. I got to the sliding door, noticed it was open, and answered the phone. It was a nurse I didn't know from the hospital, and I was told to come right away. My friend drove me back to the hospital a half-hour away. He parked the car, and when we got to the entrance, I simply became paralyzed and physically couldn't go inside. I sat on the concrete bench outside the entry doors for probably twenty minutes until I finally heard the desperate pleas of my friend to get up. I then went inside and took the elevator upstairs, knowing that my life would never, ever be the same, and walked into my mother's room. She was unconscious and breathing heavily. I was in her room for perhaps five minutes when she took her last breath and the monitor started beeping loudly. The night nurse, a kind older Japanese woman who knew my mother well, immediately came in, turned the monitor off, put her hand softly on my shoulder and said, "You know, your mom waited for you to get here so she could leave. I've seen this very often with terminal patients who should have died hours or even days before. They simply wait for their loved ones to be next to them, and then they are free to peacefully depart."

My mother's ashes, in keeping with her secular wishes, and contrary to traditional Jewish burial ceremonies, were scattered with flowers a few days later over her beloved Hawaiian blue Pacific on South Maui, a few miles from the coastline and the beach where she walked every single morning with her dear friend and next-door neighbor.

About a month later, I received a long, handwritten and heartfelt letter from the cowboy physician, who was on the mainland when my mother died. It was an incredibly touching and beautiful letter. A love letter actually, and a tribute to some of the lessons my mother had taught him about being a good doctor, and more importantly, perhaps, from his perspective, living life as a "mensch"—one of the Yiddish words she taught him—meaning a good and humane person. That wonderful letter is one of my most sacred possessions, which I still have today, safely tucked away.

The hole my mother's untimely departure left in my heart and in my life would never fully close. I also knew that my island home would never be the same without her presence. While we had many wonderful years in Hawaii surrounded by so many gentle people full of grace and kindness, I somehow intuitively knew then that I would ultimately make my life elsewhere, although I couldn't have articulated that then, nor did I know precisely why. Though I have had and am living an incredibly full and blessed life, owing much to the lessons my mother imparted and the way in which she lived her life right up to the end, I have missed her profoundly every single day of my life since.

It is true that sometimes the best-laid plans don't come to pass. Sometimes for no reason that makes any sense, sometimes for a good reason, and sometimes for a bad reason. The first, of course, is the hardest to cope with in the short term, since it seems impossible to find a place in which to "file" something which seems so incredibly unjust, although devoid of any specific malice other than, perhaps, in the case of the loss of my mother, bad gene collusion. In the long term, the need to find that "file" in which to put the unspeakable heartbreak seems to lift. And while that certainly helps ease the road to healing, going home may lead you to an entirely different place than the one you left. While it may, with the wisdom of adulthood, be wonderful to return to, it will, of course, never be the same.

4

**Every single destination, even if completely
unintended, holds the chance of
something miraculous.**

A few months after my mother died, while I was still numb and
full of excruciating grief, I flew to Tokyo in a half-hearted effort
to resume the original planned journey. My half-brother had,
during the last weeks of our mother's illness, found the prospect
of her impending death overwhelming, and rather than stay to
the end, returned to school in Europe to complete some exams.
When he was done he met me in Tokyo. After a month in Japan
visiting some friends and the host family I had lived with during
some university course work I did there, we went on to Seoul,
South Korea. I found Korea extremely interesting, though bitterly
cold in the middle of winter. In fact, the only time I remember
being warm was during the night while sleeping on traditional,
specially-heated floors in small, family-run inns. There were then
few English speakers in Korea outside of Seoul, and often the
only language I could communicate in was in Japanese, and then
only if the person was sufficiently old. Understandably, those
Koreans who could speak Japanese didn't particularly want to
do so, as war memories run long, though for the sake of helping
two often hopelessly lost Western tourists, they graciously did.

In search of warmer weather we flew on to Hong Kong, where
after about two weeks, we bought tickets to Manila. When the
plane landed at the Manila airport, I stood up, passport in hand,
grabbed my carry-on bag, then realized I had left my book on the

seat next to me. I put my passport down on the empty seat next to mine, opened my bag, put my book in, and deplaned. After waiting in what seemed like an interminable and sweltering line, we finally got to the head of the immigration desk. I reached into my purse, then realized I had left my passport on the plane. I raced back to the plane, which was already in the process of being cleaned for the return flight to Hong Kong. My passport was nowhere to be found. It had simply vanished into thin air, or, more likely, into someone else's pocket or purse. For someone who had two immigrant parents, one of whom became naturalized when I was five years old, I had always found that my passport commanded a somewhat irrational reverence from me, much like what I imagine some people feel about a treasured family Bible. Losing it somehow, on foreign soil no less, and stupidly at that, was akin in my mind to the commission of unpatriotic, blasphemous treason.

There we were at the Manila airport, and I was in effect stateless over the July 4th long holiday weekend. I called the U.S. Embassy, but could only reach a recording. Philippine immigration officials would not, of course, allow me entry, and the fact that my half-brother was traveling on his Israeli passport did not help matters any. No amount of nervous chatter was going to convince them that I was an American, despite the fact that I was born and raised in the U.S. and, unlike my half-brother, spoke unaccented English. That we had purchased one-way tickets from Hong Kong to Manila, as many young travelers did at the time, since our travels plans were fluid, did not help either. Facing the prospect of spending the long holiday weekend sleeping on hard plastic chairs at the Manila airport, I somehow managed to convince a sympathetic Philippine Airlines manager to give us a room at a hotel physically attached to the airport until Monday morning, when, ostensibly anyway, I would be able to reach an actual person with a still-beating pulse at the U.S. Embassy. Traveling on a very tight college student's budget, I was shocked when we got to the hotel room. It was an enormous suite, and the airline inexplicably and unexpectedly gave us meal vouchers for the duration of our stay. As college students accustomed to living on chump change while traveling, to us this was like hitting the proverbial lottery, especially given how it transpired. The suite also came complete with a sour-faced armed guard who looked perhaps sixteen. He was posted at our door and accompanied us angrily every time we went downstairs for a meal. We named him Attila, and though we weren't worried so much about the fall of Rome, we did have childish thoughts about a nosebleed. Monday morning finally came, and off we went, with Attila and a driver who didn't look old enough to have a driver's license, and given how he drove, probably didn't. We were unceremoniously deposited at the U.S. Embassy and handed off to a U.S. Marine guarding his post at the entry gate. Attila, it seemed, was rather pleased finally to be rid of his odd international pair of charges, and as he left gave us perhaps the only half-smile his face had ever experienced.

At the U.S. Embassy, I was also surprised to learn that I was suspected of having arrived at the Manila airport passportless because, as I later learned at that time, there was (and I imagine still is) a huge black market for used U.S. passports. The assumption was, I suppose, that as a college student I had sold mine for the then-going rate of several thousand dollars. Little did they know that personally I would have sold off a kidney to the highest bidder before I would sell my treasured passport. Once they got confirmation from officials in Hong Kong that I had had my U.S. passport as I had cleared immigration upon our departure from Kai Tak Airport, the U.S. Embassy official seemed a tad less suspicious, though still unnecessarily brusque, as if I had somehow been responsible for ruining his otherwise-perfect day. In the course of my obtaining the Hong Kong confirmation, filling out a wad of papers, getting new photographs taken and paying the replacement fee, several hours had passed. I was then given a new blue-and-gold passport, along with a rather severe admonition to hold on to this one. As if I needed to be told that!

Had this been the end of the story, two nearly broke university students—one temporarily stateless—staying in a lovely Manila airport hotel suite over a long weekend would have been miracle enough. However, the real miracle came later.

After the Manila airport debacle, we were rather anxious to leave steaming hot and crowded Manila, but it took us a few days to make arrangements. While in Manila, we stayed in a small hostel-like pension on a side street off one of the main thoroughfares; it cost three dollars a night. Breakfast and a steady supply of morbidly obese cockroaches were included. We traveled to the north, up to the incredibly beautiful scenery of Baguio, and took the infamous road to Sagada where *utterly breathtaking* doesn't do justice to the sights of the terraced rice paddies, rugged mountains and steep canyons. It is a sight that few urbanites ever get to see, and has a transformative effect. The locals we encountered were quick with bright smiles, and seemed to sing constantly. We made our way back to Manila and then flew on to Cebu City. Late one afternoon we embarked on what was supposed to be a twelve- or thirteen-hour journey on a rickety old bus which had clearly seen better days—probably several decades of better days, in either the Soviet Union or Yugoslavia. The bus, which was packed several times beyond any intended capacity, included at least a couple of dozen chickens and various other farm animals. Instead of chairs, it was fitted with thin wooden-slat benches, and had cloudy windows, several of which were broken or missing altogether. Those benches no doubt were installed to allow for maximum human and animal husbandry sardine-like capacity. That it was uncomfortable would have been the understatement of the century. But never mind, my half-brother insisted—the place we would ultimately end up, some wonderful exotic island he had heard about from some young Israeli travelers he had met in Hong Kong, with white sand beaches and thatched huts (reached ultimately via another island hop and then a sampan), would be well worth it, he assured me.

Somehow, despite the heat, the loud animal racket (as if they knew instinctively that they were destined to have a starring role at someone's family dinner), and a winding mountain road devised, I had imagined, by a civil engineer deeply addicted to opium, I managed, incredibly, to fall asleep. This was probably an act of self-preservation or an otherwise lame attempt to forget the searing pain in my derriere from the unpadded wooden bench as the bald tires of the bus bounced hard along that pitch-dark mountain road. Around two o'clock in the morning, I was jolted awake by the sound of the bus engine grinding to an ear-screeching halt. The bus then died an unceremonious death in the middle of nowhere. I remember it being so dark that I couldn't even see my hands when I put them in front of my face. Everyone climbed out of the bus. After several attempts by the driver to restart the bus, it became clear that it would go no further. We, along with everyone else, grabbed our belongings and started walking, or rather straggling, in a stumbling, sleepy manner. After a few hundred feet in the pitch-black darkness, half-dragging our bags, my half-brother the med student, a very well-traveled and normally pretty courageous guy, started having what in hindsight can only be described as a pitch-darkness-induced, nearly hysterical paranoiac panic attack. He simply started to freak out, then started mumbling that he thought we were somewhere near the region where the Muslim separatists were fighting (we weren't) and that he was traveling on an Israeli passport—as if I'd somehow managed to get sudden amnesia about his nationality. In that hellish darkness, my sleep-deprived brain went into overdrive, something I wished the bus had done instead. I then remembered that a Catholic nun had gotten on the bus just before nightfall and I didn't recall her having gotten off. I thus did what any red-blooded American Jew would do in survival mode: I forced my eyes to find her flowing habit in the darkness, and then, with a precision known mostly to experienced tailors and talented surgeons, I ensured that I stayed so close as to seem physically attached to her. I figured that if we were going to come to harm's way in a predominantly Catholic country, then we were going to do so by her side and with the benefit of her seemingly direct-dial capability to reach the local higher being.

The nun graciously took me and my now slightly calmer half-brother under her wing, and was verbally harsh with anyone who tried to bother us, the only two foreigners on that mountain road that night in the middle of nowhere. She assured us that her "convent was just up the road," and that we would be safe there until we could get another bus. I sighed with relief, although as it ultimately turned out, "just up the road" was, in reality, over four miles up the narrow mountain road, and took us nearly two hours to reach, though it seemed like forever with our bags in tow. When we finally arrived at the convent, dirty, exhausted and parched, we were greeted like expected royalty and given a shower, bottles of water and a room for the night. This was, incidentally, my first introduction to a chamber pot, which was placed strategically in the middle of our room. It was better than going out in the pitch black darkness when nature called, but perhaps not by very much. As far as we were concerned, though, this was the Philippine version of the Vatican. As I lay in the bed, I noted that this was also the first time ever that I was going to fall asleep just under a foot-long wooden crucifix hanging on the wall above the headboard of my bed. If I had ever had any doubts about the presence of a supreme higher being, that, too, was put to bed, right next to me, just under that long wooden cross.

The next morning, we were asked to join the nuns for a modest breakfast and were told then that the next bus would pass in the late afternoon. This was great they said, as it was an extra-special day at the convent, high school graduation day for the convent's orphans. And we were the guests of honor! The whole thing was surreal—the broken-down bus in the middle of nowhere, finding the nun in the dark of night, her gracious generosity toward two Western tourists, and the beautiful simplicity of the convent and the otherworldliness of the nuns and their charges. What really blew us away, though, were the "bus nun's" words as she spoke during the graduation ceremony later that day. After imparting a few words of religious inspiration to the young graduates, she thanked God for bringing the American guests safely to their convent to share in the special joy of their graduation. As I looked around at the orphans, with their toothy, bright smiles, shiny black hair, and all beaming in their clean and crisp uniforms, I became emotionally overwhelmed thinking of the sad circumstances which must have led these children to this convent orphanage, the poverty that these kids grew up with and how little opportunity it seemed they would have in the future. Despite the obvious care, love and affection these wonderful nuns had graciously bestowed upon them, these children had been, and were, for one reason or another, completely parentless in the world at the time in their lives when it mattered most.

While I was grieving deeply for the loss of my own wonderful mother, I had been one of the very lucky ones. I had been blessed with her love, guidance, counsel and spirit in my life for twenty-one years. Though far, far too short a time, it was much, much more than those smiling orphans had experienced. I thought that I might never be the same after her passing, since I was no longer someone's daughter, but perhaps I would somehow be okay. I had been given unconditional love from a generous soul, taught countless important lessons, given sufficient tools with which to make my way in the world, and various opportunities to use those tools. That revelatory experience that day in the Philippines in fact saved me, inspired me, and gave me exactly what I needed to be able to move onward with my own life, though my own loss would, to be sure, remain with me for the rest of my days.

There it was in all of its glory, a series of wholly unanticipated events and the clearly unintended and unlikely destination of a Catholic convent in the middle of nowhere where this Jewish girl's personal miracle unexpectedly arrived. I blessed that old, overstuffed, animal-packed, broken-down bus, that pitch-dark, winding mountain road, and that wonderfully gracious and generous Filipina nun and her beautiful charges. The next bus arrived later that afternoon, and away we went. Though now I had a real miracle in my pocket and in my heart with which to journey on.

5

**Stuff is just stuff. It weighs you down
sometimes to the point of paralysis.**

When I was a child, I had a quite an impressive stamp collection. For a couple of dollars from a back-of-a-magazine advertisement, I would order by mail a pile of used stamps from all over the world. Honestly, though, I think this hobby began mainly because I wanted to receive something addressed to me from the sweet old mailman who passed by our home daily carrying his big and heavy leather pouch. In the company of a world atlas, I would use specially gummed, double-folded cellophane hinges, never any glue, and place them according to country in a collector's album. There were odd monuments, different looking people and costumes, exotic locations, idyllic vistas, colorful birds and unusual animals. I would spend countless hours with my many philatelic subjects, dreaming about the countries these tiny, colorful stamps represented. It was a good way to pass some of the long and often lonely afternoons after school while I waited for my mother to arrive home from work. By the time I went on to something else, I had several encyclopedia-sized albums with thousands of stamps from over a hundred countries threatening to break the bookshelves in my bedroom.

Then there was the kitschy silver-spoon collection. I would use my meager allowance to buy a little souvenir spoon with an even smaller symbol or depiction of wherever my mother and I happened to visit. When that proved insufficient, I would endlessly hound friends and neighbors to bring me back a spoon from wherever they were going. Often, it was from a small town or place I had never heard of, like the one I received with a replica of a donut on it from "Donna's Donut Den." I'm pretty sure that no one cared about the small, one-horse town the Donut Den was located in, except, of course, for Donna. But on occasion, I would hit pay dirt. Like the time I got a really cool spoon with a cherry-red apple on it from a friend of my mother's who had gone to New York City. I was very proud of my Big Apple spoon, and imagined then riding the elevator to the top of the Empire State Building or seeing a Broadway musical. I probably had well over a hundred other spoons in my nightstand. Every time I opened or closed one of the drawers, it sounded like a particularly vicious, three-car vehicular pile up.

There were various other things I collected over the years, practically to the point of obsession and most of which I can no longer even remember. I do, however, recall that my bedroom was being overtaken by all the stuff. My desk, bookshelves and nightstands were bursting at the seams, the walls and floors were completely covered, and the space under my bed was overflowing with early teenage clutter. Getting to my bed was an obstacle course fit for military boot camp training exercises.

My mother, a hard-working and practical woman, had no use for or interest in most material things that didn't either serve a functional purpose or provide a calming aesthetic. Though always well-dressed, and wearing a single strand of white pearls, she didn't care about expensive clothes, jewelry, or most other material trappings. While she could appreciate their beauty in the abstract, she simply had no need for them. She also couldn't stand the fact that my bedroom looked like a Salvation Army dumping depot. So one day my mother came into my bedroom bunker with a large garbage bag and announced, in the middle of a balmy winter, that it was high time for spring cleaning. She said she would return in an hour to check on my progress.

When she returned, I had dutifully created two piles. One resembled a towering and majestic Mount Everest, containing the things I simply couldn't bear to part with. The second pile, which I was willing to relinquish, resembled a Lilliputian hill currently under construction by a small farm of apoplectic ants. My mother was not terribly amused by my lack of progress, so she sat down on the floor next to me, and together, we went through every single item in the Mount Everest pile. She asked me why each item was important and what memory it held for me. More often than not, my whining response to the question of why I wanted to keep it was precisely the same: "B E C A U S E." After about the twentieth B E C A U S E, we both started hysterically cracking up, practically to the point of respiratory distress. When we caught our breath, I was then able, very slowly, item by item, to dismantle the almighty Mount Everest and place its contents in the garbage bag—saving of course, the Big Apple spoon.

Recalling that day now, my mother may have been concerned about soon being unable to locate me in my bunker, so jam-packed were its contents. Either that, or she worried she would soon get an emergency call from the Department of Sanitation. But of course what she was really trying to do was to teach me something very valuable. She intuitively understood that my need to surround myself with all that stuff was really the need of an only child of a single, hard-working parent, often left alone to her own devices for long periods of time, to find some companionship and comfort among the claustrophobic clutter. The real lesson she imparted to me that day, and many times afterwards, was that the comfort I so desperately sought had to come not from material things, but from a seemingly endless reservoir which she assured me I possessed deep inside myself. My mother gently planted the seeds of realization then that all the stuff in the world would never provide me with lasting comfort or satisfaction, but only a temporary and fleeting psychological salve.

She was right, of course. And while the seduction of stuff is ever-present in our over-consuming Western society, it rarely provides more than a moment of intrinsic satisfaction. In fact, any satisfaction derived normally dissipates shortly after the tags are removed or the item is plugged in.

Over a decade later, following that awful emergency return journey to Hawaii when my mother was diagnosed as terminally ill, that important lesson once again came home to roost, not once, but twice.

After my mother passed away, I had to contend with the family home, a small cottage really, on a fairly large piece of flat land near the ocean, with tropical fruit-bearing trees my mother tended with reverence. I was just a few months out of university, and the following calendar year I was heading to a painfully expensive law school back east, thanks to a very rare full academic scholarship. After settling my mother's affairs, I had hardly any money left. Keeping the cottage, land and beloved trees was merely a pipe dream. They had to be sold. I put the cottage and adjoining land on the market with a broker, and there it sat, for three months. Not a single serious buyer. The market was way down, and I was simply hoping to pay the bank what was owed. I was starting to panic, since the balloon payment on the purchase money loan was due in a couple of months. I fired the broker. Then, with the help of a neighbor and the contents of his garage, we used bright-red spray paint and an old piece of plywood the size of a large dining room table and made a "For Sale by Owner" sign. Together my neighbor and I tied the sign with nylon rope onto the property-line fence.

I received only one call about the house and property, a few weeks after the plywood sign went up. It was from a pleasant Alaskan couple with an extended family who had been vacationing in the islands. After they confirmed that they could build an additional home on the property, they offered the full asking price, which just covered the balloon loan balance in full and the expenses of closing. The house would close escrow a month later, and the noose around my young-adult and barely solvent neck began to loosen. But I still had the contents of the little cottage with which to contend.

As I wandered in the cottage wondering what to do with the stuff—and really, there wasn't all that much, but still far more than I could take or have use for back east in microscopic graduate school housing—I ended up sitting outside under my mother's prized papaya trees. The hanging fruit was still green and would ripen just in time for the Alaskans. After a while, I got to thinking about my mother and that late afternoon ten years before with the Mount Everest pile and Lilliputian ant hill in my bedroom bunker. I tore a sweet banana from the heavily laden tree and went back inside. I put on my mother's white pearl necklace and then gathered the family photo albums and two framed pictures. One was of Madame Pele, the beautiful fire goddess of Hawaiian ancestral lore. It was thought that keeping a picture of the fierce Pele in the home would protect it. Madame Pele was definitely going with me. The other picture was a fading old photograph of Heidi, our beloved miniature Belgian Shepherd who for many years graced our lives with love, affection and devotion. Then I called the Salvation Army to come and collect everything else. A week later, I closed and locked the sliding glass front entryway to the now-empty cottage for the last time, grabbed a bunch of bananas for a neighbor, and delivered the keys to the escrow office.

A few months later, following my return to the U.S. from the Asia trip with my half-brother, I drove past the cottage. On the adjoining land, construction on the additional house was underway, and a new, fancier perimeter fence had been installed on the property. Thankfully, my mother's beloved trees were still there, proudly standing tall and bearing tropical fruit.

I shipped my belongings and the Amsterdam-purchased Volkswagen back to the west coast. Then I flew out to meet the ship and to start the long drive across the country to Washington, D.C. Though this little, dependable, economical car had been such an incredible pain in the neck when I had to depart quickly from Israel to be with my mother, it now became my personal black magic carpet to the east coast. But the car problems were far from over. I knew I wouldn't have this little car for long, but I hoped I would have it for just long enough to ride out law school in Washington, D.C.

When the little car arrived back in Long Beach from Honolulu, it was again "released" like an automotive prisoner by U.S. Customs officials, with special stickers affixed to the license plates reflecting its European genesis. I was handed a half-inch sheath of papers which made clear that I had one year from its arrival date to complete $6,000 of retrofit conversions, such as catalytic converters and other things I had no idea about, in order to enable me to register and keep the car in the U.S.

This left me with two problems. First, the car had already been on U.S. soil for nearly ten months—for the period I was with my mother, the aftermath, the duration of my Asia trip and selling the house. I could never get the costly retrofits performed in the remaining time. Second, $6,000 in conversion costs might have made sense if the little car were a $50,000 European Mercedes-Benz or a BMW, but it certainly didn't make sense for a $5,000 Volkswagen. Besides, I didn't have that kind of extra money lying around to put into a car anyway.

I entered a brave new world of customs brokers, customs agents and car mechanics, gathering an incredible amount of information useful at the time, but otherwise mind-numbingly boring. Two things were clear, though. I needed more time, and I hoped to stall the slow administrative process long enough to keep my wheels through law school. I would worry later about what would then happen to the car. So I went to the law library and, with the aid of a helpful librarian, found what I needed, and started a paper-chasing process that would end exactly three years later.

By the time I had thoroughly exhausted all of the available administrative appeals I could muster, I was one month short of law school graduation. I received an official-looking document in the mail one day which, in effect, ordered me within one week either to provide papers reflecting completion of the mandatory conversions or produce the car to be destroyed by an officially sanctioned garage. And in a rare moment of governmental efficiency, the agency provided me with a list of certified car crushers. I had no intention of making conversions I couldn't afford, and immediately made a last-ditch appeal for car clemency, or alternatively, automotive absolution. I requested that, rather than destroy a perfectly good vehicle with only 33,000 miles on its odometer, I instead be permitted to donate the car to any east coast charitable organization which could make use of it. The administrative appeals board had no doubt tired of me, and my final plea for a vehicular pardon was swiftly and summarily denied. I simply had to produce the little car for its crushing demise.

A week later, still fuming that I had to give up this perfectly good car, and couldn't even donate it to a needy charity, I drove to the duly-authorized car crusher officially sanctioned by the U.S. Customs Service in suburban Maryland. With the original bill of lading and the Order in my hand, I waited while the official car crusher finished a phone call. As I sat with my thoughts, I began to think of the intense journey this square box of metal and rubber and I had shared over many thousands of miles. Commencing in Holland, my half-brother and I had driven through Germany, Austria, Italy and Yugoslavia, along the Adriatic Sea, down to Greece, then onto the enormous and crowded ship with the little car to Limassol, Cypress, and onward to Israel, where, after two days, my life had been irrevocably altered by the news of my mother's terminal illness. That was then followed by the intense bureaucratic insanity with the car and getting it shipped out of Israel so I could get home to her in Hawaii. And then countless heartbreaking trips to the hospital as my mother's life rapidly slipped away from mine. Then back to California to attempt to learn more about my father, and the long drive across the U.S. to attend law school. To be sure, it was a monumental journey chock-full of incredible highs and wondrous international discoveries and the nearly bottomless dark pits of Purgatory.

The Car Crusher got off the phone and, without a word, I handed him the papers. He asked me a few questions about the car, and then said I would have to wait a few minutes to see the car actually being demolished. Then I would need to sign some more papers which I would then have to submit to Customs. I must have looked like a kid handing over her prized lollipop. Without a further word, he went out to the little car, then came back and told me that if I wanted, he could salvage the tires, stereo system and bucket seats and could give me $600 for those parts. I mumbled a few words of unexpected appreciation, then followed him to the damning demolition derby, signed the papers, took the cash and called for a cab.

On the way back to D.C., my thoughts returned to my mother's words about stuff so many years and a seeming lifetime before. The truth was that the little car was just a little car, but the memories, both good and bad, would remain with me. Those memories would perhaps fade or diminish over time, but unlike the car, they would never be completely demolished. The little car was gone, but the deep reservoir my mother spoke of reminded me that I got to keep what was truly important and journey onward—even if that journey was going to be on a hot and crowded subway. As I got back to D.C. later that afternoon, flush with $600 in my pocket, I thought to myself with a wry smile that the good news of the day was that at least I didn't have to search for a parking space.

Stuff is just stuff. It can clutter your life and give you a false sense of temporary and claustrophobic comfort. Homes once full of love and affection can be emptied and sold, but the memories remain. Stuff, even very useful stuff, can also be a royal pain in the neck. And sometimes, despite your very best efforts and some really dumb rules that make no rational sense to anyone with an IQ over that of a field mouse, you simply have no choice and must let go of the stuff. The coveted old Big Apple spoon and the dreams it inspired so many years ago, however, remain firmly with me. That's stuff worth keeping.

6

Educate yourself continuously.
Ignorance is highly unattractive.

Former New York Family Court Judge and later television personality Judy Sheindlin once said, "Beauty fades, but dumb is forever," then penned a book with that as its title. It made me laugh out loud when I first heard that. But there is a simple yet profound truth to that comment. At least part of it, anyway.

While I certainly agree that external beauty is temporary—just ask any aging actress scared to death of high-definition television coming to a home near you—I don't think that dumb is forever. As long as one has a still beating pulse, one can always cure dumb. Or at least make a dent in it. One need not have a PhD in anything to be smart or well-educated. Some of the smartest people I know never went to college; a few never even finished high school. I am, of course, all for formal education and higher learning. However, the school of life is of course often a fabulous and generously endowing teacher. Indeed, some of the most interesting and enlightened conversations I've had have been very far away from ivory towers or other usual places of significant intellectual discourse.

A thirty-two-year-old Muslim woman I have dealt with for several years on the Indonesian island of Lombok, a predominantly Muslim island southeast of Bali, is one of the brightest and smartest women I've ever known. Not atypically for women in that region, her formal education ended in the 8th grade. She and the dozen village women with whom she oversees the harvesting, stringing and selling of pearl jewelry to tourists do not among them have a full set of teeth. She does, however, speak six languages fluently, conducts business with wholesalers around the globe with an iron-laced glove, owns a plot of land on which she has built a comfortable and spotless home, and supports a large extended family on her earnings. She also sends her two young sons to expensive private schools and can talk long into the night (and we have) on a multitude of interesting subjects with remarkable insight and clarity. On my last trip to Indonesia, I finally got the courage to talk with her about religion, as she has never in my presence worn a head scarf or body covering. She told me that she and her Muslim husband were "happy with their God and often went to the local mosque to hear their leaders speak, but were not fanatic," and that her husband told her fourteen years ago just as they were getting married that "she should do she wants." Hence, she has never worn a head scarf or body covering outside of a mosque, though she is, she insists "proud of her Muslimness."

I had heard that the new international airport on Lombok scheduled to open in late 2011 (or, more realistically, late 2012 or beyond, given the snail's pace of the construction's progress), was bankrolled entirely by the Saudis, to the tune of $600 million. Treading lightly, I cautiously asked her if this would have any collateral religious effect on the island. She insisted the airport was funded by Dubai money, not Saudi money, despite articles in the international press and confirmation of foreign expatriates to the contrary. She added that while she was happy about the prospect of more tourism and consequent potential income that might result, she was concerned that the rampant corruption which is part and parcel of everyday life in Indonesia would in reality not provide any additional income to the everyday people such as herself. Instead, it would simply add to the personal pockets of the well-connected. She also told me that she did not believe the presence of tourists from the Middle East would have any religious impact on the local Muslims or their lifestyle.

While I believe without hesitation the societal threat posed by corruption, I am less convinced that the local lifestyle of the place will remain unchanged by Middle-Eastern influence. If what has transpired on the island of Bali is any indication, in a few short years, life on Lombok will be irretrievably altered, and most likely not for the better. I am not saying at all that Lombok or any other place in the world should remain in an underdeveloped time warp; on the contrary. However, if you take an excruciatingly painful lack of intelligent urban planning, and rabid, nearly unregulated development on every inch of vacant land without any regard whatsoever to the limited civil and administrative infrastructure; then you mix in rampant, officially condoned corruption from high up the political ladder all the way down to the local police force; and then stir in a largely undereducated and impoverished population—you have a recipe for a very dangerous future course. Especially where religion gets involved. If only the local population had access to more readily available and inexpensive educational opportunities. And if that does come to pass, and I truly hope it does in the near future, I will personally pray to all textbooks that those educational opportunities and the books they feature are secular in nature. I can only hope that intelligent people like my Muslim friend can make their voices heard among all the competing interests of the archipelago and beyond.

Recently, I took a taxi from a friend's home in Singapore to the airport. Normally, I would take the MRT, Singapore's high-tech metro system, which is spotless, stunningly efficient and drops one off at an international airport of a traveler's dreams. But on that eighty-five degree, eighty-percent-humidity day, I just couldn't bear the heat and called a cab. Singapore, with the constant construction going on around the clock and the massive MRT extension to all corners of the island city-state, performed for the most part by laborers imported mainly from Sri Lanka and India, is well-known for its parking-lot-like traffic. But all I could think of that afternoon was extremely frigid air

37

conditioning. With typical Singaporean efficiency, the taxi came on time, and (heaven bless ice-cold refrigeration), the cab was like a hotel kitchen meat locker. Driving me was a Singaporean Chinese man of about forty. To sum up, that was one of most interesting and enlightened conversations I have ever had. He was well-educated, spoke excellent, heavily-accented English, and knew as much about the world as anyone with whom I had recently spoken.

If that Singaporean cab driver wasn't at least college educated, then he must have spent every waking hour he wasn't in his cab voraciously reading anything he could get his hands on. Among other things, we discussed Hong Kong and my perception that things were actually much better there after Britain's ninety-nine-year lease expired and it was returned to China. Certainly it was much cleaner, the ubiquitous, ever-present smoking had been contained to a large extent, and construction continued at a frenetic pace, with office buildings and five-star hotels going up on reclamation lands in West Kowloon at a dizzying pace. I recalled just prior to the British handover that I was really worried that things would go south in Hong Kong, a city I really loved and in which I had spent a lot of time over the years, and where I had several good friends. Obviously I was not alone in these worries as, just before the handover, thousands of Hong Kong residents frantically sought out whatever foreign passports were available to them. Thankfully, most of those fears did not come to pass. The cabdriver told me that "he was pleased that China had behaved well in Hong Kong following the handover and that it gave him high hopes for Taiwan." That thought threw me for a complete loop as, although I consider myself fairly well-read about the region, I had never heard any serious discussion of China truly playing a larger role in Taiwan, an ethnically Chinese island nation with a long and fairly antagonistic history with its mainland cousins. If what this cab driver posited were true, what would that look like? Especially given the way China has dealt so harshly with Tibet. At least with Taiwan, there would be no issue of national language suppression I thought. I took the cab driver's pearl of wisdom and decided that if what he said were true and came to pass, I would likewise have to hope for "good behavior."

We also spoke of my daughter's Chinese language studies in Singapore. He said that "that was really great, because in the future big business would be conducted worldwide in only two languages, English and Chinese." That was probably a true statement.

It's just remarkable just how much changes in a generation. When I was growing up, everything, it seemed, was "Made in Japan," and when I was in college and entering the work force, the language to learn was Japanese. So that was the language I studied, and, in fact, it was the only foreign language I formally studied—though I had a bit of an edge, since about forty percent of Hawaii's population was Japanese, and one of my mother's closest friends, who lived next door, was of Japanese descent and spoke it well. I spent countless hours with her and her family over the years, as did our daughter when she was young. Thus I was familiar and comfortable with the culture and its music, and had an ear and an affinity for the language by the time my serious studies commenced. Now, of course, it seems everything is "Made in China."

For the first time ever, I was deeply saddened that on that particular day, for some inexplicable reason, there was very little traffic in Singapore, and my fascinating cab driver made it to the airport in near-record time, just under a half hour. He jumped out of the cab, retrieved my luggage "from the boot," put it by the entry door and, much to my surprise, held his hand out and shook mine vigorously with both of his and thanked *me*, telling me that this was one of the most pleasurable rides he could remember. I told him the pleasure was all mine, and it most certainly was. I then turned to re-enter one of the greatest airports in the world, complete with ice-cold air conditioning.

On the flipside, ignorance is most certainly neither cash specific nor indicative of one's education or station in life.

I have met many, many people with all kinds of financial wealth and freedom out of whose mouths unspeakable ignorance was uttered. A couple of particularly remarkable stories come to mind.

I once brought a lobbyist with very strong China ties to a firm I was with, as the lobbyist was seeking a U.S. based law firm to facilitate some business he had in the works. The senior partner, whose last name graced the firm's letterhead, joined us for that introductory meeting. The lobbyist did what most lobbyists do, namely talked about his vast connections and what he hoped to achieve in the next few years and what his needs would be going forward with a law firm. Every so often he would say something was "ten million RMB" or refer to a project that was "one hundred million RMB." After about half an hour, the lobbyist's cell phone rang, and, as it was a call from Beijing, he answered it. While the lobbyist was on the phone, the senior partner leaned over to me and whispered, "Why the hell does this guy keep talking about rhythm and blues? I don't know jack shit about music, and what the hell does that have to do with China anyway?" It was all I could do not to crack up out loud in the partner's face. The partner may not have known squat about music, but he also didn't know a thing about foreign currency, or indeed even the name of the currency of one of the largest economies in the world. Though he was more than happy to earn money from this lobbyist. I found that to be a very sorry state of affairs, and highly unattractive. It was no surprise to me that the lobbyist didn't hire the law firm for his needs.

My mother, who spoke excellent English although she never lost her throaty accent, was often asked where she was from by various people during the span of the twenty-three years she lived in the U.S. Often the responses to her statement that she was originally from Israel were hilarious. One person said, "How interesting! I have always loved spaghetti." She was referring, we assumed, to Italy, though the famous noodle actually originally hailed from China. Another person said, "I would like to go there someday and play golf but I heard it rains a lot there." This was hysterical as up until 1999 there was only one lonely and fairly lousy golf course in the entire state of Israel. Now there are all of two. And rain in the desert is a rather rare and quite precious commodity. Wet and golf-course-studded Ireland, however, is only a continent away. And yet another responded, "So you speak Israelian too?" Our perennial favorite though was from a bank manager who said, "You must get a break on the price of gas since your country has so much oil." That one just about rendered my quick-witted mother speechless, since, of course, there isn't a single drop of black gold anywhere to be found in Israel, though Iraq is sort of nearby. Apparently the common thread was reminiscent of categories on the popular prime-time game show Jeopardy: "Name countries that start with the letter 'I'."

While these comments were sometimes stunningly funny, they also indicated a fairly unattractive ignorance of those who uttered them; though their ilk is certainly not elicited only by Israel. People from many other countries are often faced with similar ignorance or worse. Of course, one doesn't need a passport or even the desire for international travel to have a basic understanding of the planet and its inhabitants. Just a library card and regular reading of a newspaper will suffice. I love this country profoundly, and I am not American-bashing; however some Americans' center-of-the-universe concept, accompanied by very little general understanding of other countries, their languages, geography, religion and resources, and their importance to the world stage, is often pretty scary— not to mention potentially dangerous on the political world stage.

You never know where and from whom you will gain great insight or get the best education. It may not always come from a professor in an ivory tower or from a Wall Street guru, but from places and people you least expect. When that wisdom is shared, it is an incredible gift, and the person bestowing its blessing becomes as beautiful as Cinderella or as handsome as a prince on a white horse. So I say to the Honorable Judge Judy, take heart—things are not always what they seem. While beauty may in fact be temporary, dumb can be, too. And hopefully will be. A wonderful surprise gift of insight or wisdom may be just around the corner in the most unlikely place imaginable. Or it may be in the local library. And it may very well be beautiful and permanent.

7

Maintain your personal temple. Keep fit, in any way you enjoy.

I remember now with comical clarity the Jane Fonda-style leggings of the late 1970s and 80s, mostly because I owned several neon-colored pairs of them. They had to match the extremely snug Lycra leotards that were cut so high on the thigh, nearly to the side of the waist. Then, of course, there was the really big hair. I had just started college and was working nearly full-time, and these aerobic classes were a good way to unload enough stress to permit me to study hard enough to get the grades I wanted and needed to get. We all looked ridiculous in those get-ups as we huffed and puffed our way to an obscenely loud, musically induced state of sweaty aerobic Zen.

Utterly laughable attire aside, Jane Fonda was clearly on to something. That she brought it to the masses with highly commercialized VHS tapes (now I'm REALLY dating myself) and made a lot of money from the endeavor is completely beside the point. One only needs to look at her now, well into her eighth decade, to see that she remains vital, vibrant, fit and attractive. Her life long exercise regimen clearly has physically paid off well for her.

My own exercise journey began one school morning in 1969. Inexplicably, I woke up very early, and with no forewarning whatsoever, scrounged under my bed for my prized red Keds, and made my way to the front door. My mother, in the kitchen of our small house, holding the proverbial cup of mud-like coffee that was nearly perpetually in her hand, asked where I was going at that early hour. I told her I was going to start the day by going running. With a thoroughly perplexed look on her face, she asked very seriously in her heavily accented English, "But who on earth are you running from?" I laughed and tossed the comment aside in a nine-year-old's perception of the vast generational and cultural divide that seemingly existed between us and went out the front door.

That first twenty minute run, or rather limp-along jog on cracked pavement with lousy shoes, marked the beginning of a lifetime of exercise. I never became a long-distance runner, mainly because of boredom; indeed, the longest I ever ran was a half-marathon in Honolulu while at university. That was enough for me. But I ran four or five miles a day in the lush hills of Manoa all through those university days, in addition to taking those Fonda-esque classes, as an easy and cheap method of staying fit, both physically and mentally.

Over the years it seems that I have tried practically everything. Surfing, ballet, gymnastics, weight lifting, tennis, snorkeling, scuba diving, cardio training, and in my late thirties and early forties, kick-boxing. It became the rage of the day owing mainly to Billy Blanks, a soft-spoken and seemingly religious man who started his climb to popularity in a dumpy garage deep in the bowels of the San Fernando Valley of Southern California. He pioneered a form of kick-boxing known as Tae Bo, and rapidly rose to fame, though relatively short-lived, even by L.A. standards. He ended up with an enormous air-conditioned studio in a swankier part of town manned almost entirely by his several brothers and sisters and extended family members. His studio came complete with personal trainers, baby-sitting services and religious quotations painted on the walls in letters so large that even those deemed legally blind couldn't miss them. The studio was a veritable one-stop shopping arcade for physical stamina, good health, fruit juice and religious possibilities. Then came his exercise DVD's, the infomercials, and then the obligatory cameos in a few popular prime-time television shows. He became a household name in the exercise arena in those days, at least in Southern California. Until, that is, as I'd heard from one of his former instructors, he went to Japan several years ago on an Asian marketing blitzkrieg, impregnated his Japanese interpreter and then left his American wife of many, many years who had been with him since the dumpy old garage days. He is apparently now all the rage in Japan. Admittedly, while attending his classes, I was in the best physical shape of my entire life. I attained a toned and hard-bodied, state of blissful physical Nirvana, without the religion.

Since those days, there has been bike riding, spinning, more tennis, Pilates, yoga, hip-hop, and some hybrid classes, such as cardio barre, which meshed several exercise concepts together. Indeed today there are more types of classes at local health clubs then there are types of cheese in France. For now I have mainly a steady diet of spinning, cardio core and tennis, with the occasional jog or yoga class thrown in for good measure.

Saying that exercise has gotten me through some tough times simply wouldn't be a fair statement. I believe it has allowed me to lead a much happier, less-stressful and healthier life. During particularly stressful times of personal crisis, while cramming and sitting for the Bar exam, or, later, working ungodly hours on high-pressure deals at large law firms under the tutelage of some fairly miserable people, exercise was my personal salvation and my savior. It became not a luxury for possessing good form, but an absolute necessity for maintaining any semblance of mental health. That said, I am not an exercise addict, though my husband might argue otherwise, as I usually exercise six days a week when at home with a slight touch of religious fervor. As I write this chapter, I've been on the road in Asia now for three weeks. While I probably have walked a hundred-plus often-circular urban miles though many of my old haunts, I've been to a "real" gym only twice, once in Hong Kong and once in Singapore. I also attended only one yoga class in Indonesia, which I didn't particularly enjoy. This was mainly because the instructor seemed to be about twelve and really didn't have a clue as to what he was doing. But it didn't matter. The 'instructor' was friendly, at least, the class was outside, the weather was good, and the ubiquitous and relentless Indonesian mosquitoes were inexplicably absent for the class's duration. Afterwards, you could simply roll into the bathtub temperature swimming pool. An altogether delightful experience, the untrained, smiling, teenaged boy/man notwithstanding.

When I get home I will undoubtedly go back to my six-days-a-week, fairly intense routine. Not out of a sense of a physical mandate, though admittedly there is that also to a certain degree, but more because it contributes in a myriad of untold ways to a general sense of mental well-being. Countless times over the years when faced with a seemingly insurmountable problem—little kids, little problems, big kids, bigger problems—or a plethora of mammoth work-related crises upon which were riding several million dollars of other people's money, it all simply seemed more manageable following a lunch hour at the gym, or simply a brisk walk around the block in the company of a four-legged fur person.

Find something to do—anything at all—and preferably outside, that floats your boat, or at least allows you some time to escape the cacophony of noises vying for your constant attention. And, as the brilliant marketing team at Nike Corporation said, "Just do it." Your body and mind, and most likely your friends, family, and co-workers, will thank you.

8

Wear other people's shoes. They may never fit, but the insight will be invaluable.

This has been an exercise I've engaged in many times over the years as I've tried to make sense of things which, in general, made no sense to me at all.

Take something as simple as an incident in which someone treats you badly, when you feel you've done nothing to deserve it. Put on their shoes. Or something much more complex—for example, fundamental lifestyle or religious differences that are often much harder to understand or accept, despite the best of intentions. Try on their shoes.

During a trip to Malaysia about five years ago, and again more recently in Indonesia, both predominantly Muslim countries, it was very difficult for me to see full-chador-clad Muslim women—several women to one man—on the beaches, not just walking, but entering the water with those heavy dark robes and head scarves. Frankly, and simply as a practical matter, I often feared they would drown with all that wet, heavy material, especially in what can be rather strong currents and undertows. I should note here that none of these women I saw, in either Malaysia or Indonesia, seemed unhappy; indeed they all appeared to be enjoying themselves immensely in the presence of what was invariably a lone man wearing surfer-style board shorts and nothing else. To me, the disparity between the women's and men's dress seemed incongruous and patently unfair. Religious notions of female piety firmly aside, having spent so much of my fifty years in, at or near an ocean, it's very hard for me to imagine what it must be like not to feel the salty, warm, crystal-clear water lapping against one's head or body, or the heat of a mid-summer sun on one's back, or not to be able to swim freely in clear, blue water. And to a Westerner's eyes, these burdensome coverings must, by definition, preclude altogether engaging in any kind of underwater activity or water sports.

Perhaps these women's lives were so full and so satiated with other things that they didn't feel deprived of those opportunities which have always been readily available to my generation and those following and which are all so easily taken for granted. Perhaps it is they who view us scant bikini-clad and non-husband-sharing women as the ones who are lacking or otherwise deprived, morally and otherwise. It is hard to say without delving into the even more complex religious and social issues surrounding the covering of women in traditional Muslim societies. I read awhile back that a group of women in Saudi Arabia staged, through Facebook, a minor revolt again the Saudi ban on women driving. These courageous women, wearing the traditional, black *abaya* and thus covered from head to toe, got into their respective cars at different places in the capital city of Riyadh and simply drove. Several were consequently arrested and reported that they were simply fed up with having to depend on male drivers to get around. And they said this desire had nothing to do with religion. Perhaps there will be a similar occurrence with the head and body coverings one day. Or maybe not.

Recently I was at a dinner party in Benoa, Indonesia to which I was invited by a Frenchwoman I had met over a decade earlier at Orly Airport in Paris en route to Agadir, Morocco. Our then three-year-old daughter offered a lollipop to her seven-year-old daughter, and we have been great friends ever since. We stayed in touch over the years, meeting up in Paris when we both happened to be there, or in Indonesia, where she has lived for the past two decades. At this dinner party, just a few days before Bastille Day, there were several expatriate French couples—a

Frenchwoman and her Javanese husband, the Balinese boyfriend of my girlfriend, my girlfriend's now college-aged daughter, *her* French boyfriend and me. It was a pretty colorful group, as most expatriate gatherings are, replete not just with French expats, but the widest varieties of backgrounds imaginable. Getting the back story of the French/Javanese couple over a pastis before the party started, I learned that the man had another wife, who was Muslim, living on Java, with whom he had four kids, ages six to sixteen, and whom he visited twice a month. The Frenchwoman and Javanese man had no children together.

Even more amazing to me, during the previous school holidays, the Javanese man had brought his and wife-number-one's four children to Bali for a holiday with the understanding that wife-number-two would watch the children while he was at work. This Frenchwoman is attractive, intelligent, pleasant and very successful in her profession, owns a home on Bali, and is financially secure in her own right. The Javanese man was likewise very pleasant and animatedly charming. However as he and my girlfriend's Balinese boyfriend were the only two non-French-speakers there that evening, and the rest of us, out of unconscious habit, constantly reverted back to French, he and his French wife-number-two left shortly after dessert.

After the party, I spoke to my girlfriend at length about the French/Javanese couple. She said she really didn't understand why the Frenchwoman stayed with the Javanese man under these circumstances, and she fully agreed with me as to this woman's considerable talents and strengths. My girlfriend continued to shake her head as we straightened up and then said, "It's sad—I think that she simply cannot be alone."

We all know there are a million incredible stories out there. Husbands and wives and illicit affairs, one-night stands and long-term mistresses, illegitimate children and even hidden teenagers born to long-term domestic help—gasp—as was exposed a few months ago by California's former governor. Secrets abound of as many colors, shapes, lengths and varieties as there are stars in the sky. But I think what made the French/Javanese couple's story so hard for me grasp, her shoes so difficult for me to step into, was that the duplicity, or rather the affront I perceived to Western women's notions of reason and fairness, was so overt and out in the open.

Over the next couple of days I mulled this story over in my mind, trying to make some sense of it. Along the way, I realized three things. First, I knew virtually nothing about this Frenchwoman's life before she came to Indonesia and what made her who she became, and so accepting of a situation most, if not all, Western women wouldn't be able to tolerate for a New York minute. Second, I realized that while I could try on her ill-fitting and fairly uncomfortable shoes, I actually didn't need to make sense of it or have those shoes fit me. It was her life and hers alone in which to choose to be happy or miserable. It was enough that I tried, even momentarily, to step into those shoes. Third, and perhaps most interesting to me, was that the Frenchwoman's situation and lifestyle choices gave me pause, just long enough for me once again to contemplate what I call the "accident of birth" theory and what that means in relation to the opportunities women typically have or are accorded in the places in which they just happen to be born, and what they are able do with those choices.

My mother was born in a time and place where the typical path of young women was fairly pre-ordained. She had a life script imposed by family and society; a relatively insignificant job following high school, followed by marriage, the end of that meaningless job, and onto the more important job of raising children. Deviating from that narrowly defined script became my mother's mission. She desperately wanted to be a physician, and was good in the requisite math and sciences. However, her father wouldn't hear of it. To him, it was simply unacceptable, as he feared that her being a physician would make her unmarriageable, a fate, in his opinion, that was practically tantamount to death. After heated family debates over the course of several months in which her own mother was unable, because of the authoritarian pecking order, to participate, my mother and her father reached what was, to my mother, an "unsatisfactory compromise, but better than the alternative of nothing." She would go to a special school, which had courses in foreign languages, administrative policy and public administration. Why her father thought this course of study would make my mother more marriageable than medicine remains one of my family's big unanswered mysteries. Though perhaps tongue-in-cheek, this had to do with the fact that policy and administrative personnel don't regularly see people naked; at least in the literal sense.

As it turned out, this path led my mother to a fairly satisfying career in the Israeli Foreign Service and provided her with an ability to see the world and engage in very interesting work. And this was a good thing from a purely selfish perspective, since it resulted in her ultimately meeting my father in the U.S. and my consequent birth. However, my mother's desire to be a physician never really left her. After she retired from her work with the IFS when she was in her late thirties, she felt she was too old and had too many responsibilities for medical school. So she enrolled in nursing school instead and went on to a fairly satisfying second career in the psychiatric field. She was still left, though, with lingering thoughts, as many of us are, about the roads she was unable to travel because of the "accident of birth" theory. This is one reason perhaps, why the Frenchwoman's story in Benoa was so bothersome to me. She had all of the opportunities afforded to her, yet inexplicably chose a path few Western women would have selected. But perhaps that was exactly the point I was altogether missing: the Frenchwoman had opportunities and choices and simply made her own decisions, for whatever reasons made sense to her. And that simply had to be enough for me.

As to more mundane (but nevertheless significant to me) matters, on that same Asia trip, I was having lunch while reading a book at a traditional Indonesian *warung*, an open-air eatery serving local food, in Kuta on a miniscule, perhaps thirty-foot, allegedly one-way road. It was really more of a dense commercial alleyway running perpendicular to a main thoroughfare that faced the beach. As driving rules are virtually non-existent in Indonesia, the concept of one-way streets has not yet really taken any degree of hold, despite the presence of signage. As I was eating, I saw this young, pretty and well-groomed mother exit a mini-market across the street from where I was sitting, with her three children in tow, all of them probably under the age of five. On that hot day, each of the three children was holding with reverence an ice cream that she had just bought for them. The other hand was either holding the mother's hand or that of one of the other children. The mother and her charges then very carefully, hand-in-hand, crossed this street, packed with motorcycles speeding along and pedestrians trying to walk without getting maimed or worse, along with the occasional car or truck trying to squeeze through. They successfully made their way to other side of the street and I exhaled a sigh of relief. It was just about as I went back to my plate of chicken satay that I saw her load all three of the children on a man's motorcycle—with no helmets, of course—and watch as they sped away in the hot mid-day sun. She walked the other direction, to take care, I imagined, of some errands or shopping. I didn't know whether to laugh or cry, so overwhelming was the irony of safe passage across a suicide-style alley, only to have four people pile onto an old motorcycle in an incredibly crowded and congested city known for some of the scariest driving on planet earth.

To be sure, Indonesia is not alone in this matter of death-defying driving. While in Ho Chi Minh City with our daughter in 2005, I thought I would either die or become eligible for social security benefits long before I could cross the main roadways, so jam-packed with motorcycles were the inner-city streets. Finally, deciding anything was better than having heat stroke while traveling, I simply did what the locals did, namely held out my arm at waist height, gesturing "don't you *dare* run me over," and crossed the street. The difference between the locals and me, I imagine, is that while crossing, I engaged in multi-lingual prayers to any higher being who might be listening or otherwise available. All over Vietnam one can see entire families, sometimes four or five deep, and countless babies on board one small motorcycle. Or two people carrying an impossible amount of cargo several feet wide extending heavily off of both sides of a motorcycle defying all potential laws that Sir Isaac Newton could possibly have theorized. The most comically improbable one I saw was the transporting of at least twenty dozen flats of eggs, strapped to a motor cycle criss-crossed with colorful bungee cords. I also regularly saw animals being transported this way. Not chickens or other small animals, though there were plenty of those being transported too, but I regularly saw large cows moved this way, upside down, with their hooves tied together on a stick of bamboo. All notions of non-existent statutes regarding decent animal husbandry aside.

But the image of the Indonesian mother and her three children somehow stuck with me. Here too I had to step out of my shoes and attempt to step into hers. From my rule-infested, urban-American point of view, this was, plain and simple, total insanity. Although admittedly, more than once I hopped on a Vietnamese motorcycle "taxi" when that was all that was available and the heat became overwhelming. And in a never-to-be repeated moment of temporary insanity, in Indonesia in 2006, I once carried three oversized canvas paintings from the studio of a local artist on the back of what seemed like a five-horsepower motorcycle as the driver maneuvered over obscenely deep pot holes back to my bungalow several miles away. Though slightly tongue-in-cheek, two of those canvases contained painted images of Buddha, and perhaps that saved me from either the pot holes as large as end tables or carbon monoxide poisoning. I may never recover from that experience. But as I said earlier, I have done some pretty stupid things in fifty years. For the Indonesian mother, however, it was just another day. She got her children ice cream, assured her and their safe passage across the crowded alley, then did what everyone there does, namely put them on motorcycles without helmets and sent them on their way while she did what she needed to do.

Some people's shoes can be worn temporarily where ever you happen to be. At home as you attempt to go about your business without stepping on other's feet, or try to deal with those who seem to have stepped on yours. Or far away from home as you maneuver societal norms, cultural conflict or ideas simply different from your own. Those other shoes may never, ever fit you. Indeed, they may bother you immensely, be bizarre, risky or simply hurt like hell. But it is important to try those shoes on and walk about a bit in order to ascertain and determine precisely the type and kind of shoes which are right for you. In so doing, hopefully you will get from point A to point B with all of your body parts intact and also gain a glimmer of understanding that your shoes, which fit snugly and feel more comfortable—which, in fact, feel like old shoes—just aren't the same shoes or even worn in the same way, as those in much of the world. And that has to be just fine.

9

Don't wear shoes in the house.
Literally or figuratively.

To anyone growing up in Hawaii, at least in my generation, wearing shoes in the house was strictly verboten. Part Asian influence, part island lifestyle, removing one's shoes at the door was simply the local custom. No one gave much thought to its cultural genesis. It was just a habit that occurred every single day. As a result, despite sand and salt water and other beach detritus everywhere, the inside of people's homes was always pretty clean. The big problem at large social gatherings, though, was leaving with the same pair of shoes with which you arrived. Or often, leaving with any shoes at all. I remember more than once leaving with men's sandals because someone had inadvertently walked off with mine and I couldn't squeeze my size 7½ foot into the mostly size 5 women's shoes left by the door. Thus, cheap, easily replaceable flip flops were the order of the day. Socks and "real" shoes were only worn in the dead of winter, when the thermometer dipped to a chilly seventy degrees and sweat pants were likewise hauled out of the winter closet.

As a result, when I moved to Japan, the transition to shoeless household living came easily and made perfect sense, given the traditional tatami-mat rooms many homes there still possessed at the time. The Japanese have also a seemingly national cultural pride about their household cleanliness. Not only did I not ever see anything resembling a shoe in a house or apartment other than a soft bedroom-style slipper, I also never once saw an unkempt home or apartment.

Also, in Paris, where I lived in the early 1990s, many people removed their shoes at the entryway. That, of course, was long before people started picking up after their beloved dogs, those furry friends who often perceived the glorious City of Lights as the largest fire hydrant in the canine free world. Thankfully, with the enactment of several doggy-detritus city ordinances, things are much better now in that regard. Though one can still go practically everywhere in Paris with four-legged family members. And by "everywhere" I mean five-star hotels and restaurants, subways, buses, trains, churches, the post office and virtually every government office a civilian might need to enter. However, despite the charming, often irrationally close relationship the French have with their beloved dogs, Parisians in particular have become far more conscious of having their beautiful city be poop-free. And those of us who love to walk Paris with a fervor akin to that of having a religious experience are grateful for this new-found affection for plastic bags and attention to trash receptacles.

Maintaining a household shoe-free existence in Southern California, however, has proved to be far more of a challenge when some people routinely spend the annual gross domestic product of Bangladesh on one pair of high-style Manolo Blaniks. Asking them to remove their shoes and leave them by the front door, even *inside,* would simply be social suicide. So I have had to make shoe compromises when guests come over—namely, no shoes upstairs. This seems to work out just fine; our friends can laugh at my shoe quirkiness if they want to go upstairs, and I can laugh too while I get to enjoy the spotlessly clean upstairs. Win, win.

There is something to be said about not wearing shoes at home. The outside world is the outside world, and who wants all that dirt—and worse—inside your home anyway? The very same place where you often frolic on the floor or carpet with your kids and dogs or watch a movie with a bowl of popcorn propped on a big pillow? The shoeless-at-home concept always seemed rather comical to my husband, who routinely reminds me that I own more shoes than there are people living in East Timor. Years ago, before I, pardon the pun, pared down, I was flippantly compared to the now-infamous Imelda Marcos, I had so many shoes. The former first lady of the Philippines was rumored to have *thrice* the number of pairs of shoes than people living in East Timor while her own people languished in abject poverty. What was Imelda going to do with all those shoes anyway? Pull a Marie Antoinette and tell the hungry Philippine population to wear shoes when what they really needed was food?

That is the literal shoe story. But there is, of course, a figurative shoe story as well. The house as home and hearth is, as the old saying goes, where the heart is. Shoes as a metaphor should be removed and left at the proverbial front door upon entry when we communicate and deal with people in our homes. Our homes ideally should be a place of refuge, sanctuary, relaxation and peacefulness. In order to deal successfully with the outside world and all that it entails, we are constantly wearing layer upon layer of often-necessary psychological armor in order to deal with colleagues, co-workers, judges, opponents, medical professionals, PTA members, coaches, referees, teachers, the mailman, the gardener, the grocer, the plumber, and on and on. In the sanctity of our homes, however, the protections and survival mechanisms we sometimes need in order to survive and thrive in our often-complicated and hurried world should not, even in an imperfect world, be necessary. Thus, if you feel the need to put your figurative shoes on in order to communicate or deal with those you invite into your home or those with whom you live and love, then you (or they) should be at the front door, ready to leave. And in order to facilitate a sense of household calm, you may, just slightly tongue-in-cheek, want to point those shoes toward the outside, though away a bit from the front door. Feng Shui masters have long said that shoes too close to the front door constitute clutter and create stagnant energy (chi). Perhaps that will help restore some calm at home. It certainly can't hurt.

10

Live with animals. The four-legged variety.

Although much was made of John Grogan's well-written and often hilarious book *Marley & Me*, there are countless other wonderful stories about dogs and their human friends.

For as long as I can remember there was always a dog in my home. First there was Freddy the black schnauzer, who made breakfast, lunch, hors d'oeuvres, afternoon tea, dinner and dessert out of my mother's intimate laundry hanging tantalizingly from the backyard clothes line. Needless to say, sweet little Freddy did not last long in our home. Freddy was followed by Heidi, a miniature Belgian Shepherd. Heidi was part of our family for nearly fourteen years. She was, by all accounts, a true shepherd: loyal, gentle, and smarter than many humans I know. She was also one of the best and fondest parts of my childhood. I can't say enough about what it means for a child, especially one growing up as an only child, to have a perpetual best friend, always readily available to give and receive all that wet-nosed, slurpy-tongued, dirty-pawed love and affection. Dogs provide a stable force of continuous and unconditional love in an often distracting and confusing world.

When I went off to college, away from home, and then graduate school 7,000 miles away, I had several living arrangements. First a dorm, then a shared apartment, then a shared house, then finally an apartment all to myself. In none of those places could I have a dog. And even if I could have, it wouldn't have been fair to the animal as I was always too busy to care for a dog. I always felt that, no matter how much I enjoyed those places and the people I was with, the apartment or house never really felt like a home without a wagging tail cruising around.

When in 1992 I was finally in a situation where I felt I could have a dog, I did just that. I went to the local pound and got a gray terrier puppy whom I immediately named Pauillac, after a place I had enjoyed being one summer in France. The name cracked me up, and I thought that while I could never curse a child with such a funny name, I could certainly do so with a dog. I mean, would a dog ever really get a complex over a weird name? And if it did, would it care? Naming a dog Pauillac in France was just like naming a dog Fresno in California. The town of Pauillac, far and away, certainly has better wine, not to mention cheese and bread and foie gras, than Fresno could ever dream of having. Though I've heard there are some decent onions in Fresno.

Pauillac had been found alone roaming the streets, I was told by the kind-hearted guy at the shelter. She had, I learned when I tried to take her to my car, never been on a leash. And she had certainly never been up or down a flight of stairs. Trying to get that dog to go up the stairs to the condominium I was in took over an hour. And I failed miserably. My frustration got the best of me and I finally carried the dirty little pooch up the stairs. I also found out, following her bath, that Pauillac wasn't gray at all, but snow white.

Poor Pauillac had every possible ailment a street dog could have had. She had a severe case of intestinal worms, near-terminal fleas, and ear mites, just to name a few. My kitchen, where Pauillac was sleeping the first couple of weeks, resembled a miniature veterinary hospital unit on steroids. But through it all, Pauillac seemed so happy to have been rescued that she endured the seemingly endless cornucopia of medicine and treatments. Then Pauillac got healthy, and she went from very happy to positively ecstatic. That unadulterated and beaming joy never left her for a minute until the day eighteen years later when she wagged her tail for the very last time.

Pauillac finally did get leash-trained and learned to maneuver stairs, ultimately with the reckless abandon of the truly insane. In fact, her favorite form of exercise besides her daily walks was running up and down the stairs in a sort of self-induced frenzy for no good reason that I could come up with other than the entirely Zen concept that the stairs were simply there. Put there, I'm sure she thought, for her cardio pleasure and hers alone, never mind that anyone happened to sleep nearby.

Like Marley, Pauillac committed so many mischievous acts over the years that I lost count, mostly because I couldn't count that high without an abacus. There were the "usual" terrier (read "terror") acts, like leaving dead birds as presents by my bedroom door. I will never forget the head tilt and look of utter confusion Pauillac had on her face when I wasn't nearly as happy about the dead bird as she was thrilled to show me the fruits of her canine labor while I slumbered.

Then there were the more ridiculous incidents. On the afternoon before I was having ten people over for dinner, I was putting the final touches on three large deep-dish Pyrex plates of home-made lasagna, then covered them and put them carefully in the refrigerator and left for the wine shop. Apparently I didn't close the refrigerator door strongly enough to make a firm seal. It was a beautiful sunny day, and I took a short walk after leaving the wine shop, arriving home around five in time to put the lasagna in the oven. I walked into the kitchen and my first thought was that I had inadvertently walked into a MASH unit following a North Korean blitz. I fully expected Alan Alda to saunter in with a scalpel and a vodka martini, or at least Alan Funt to come in with a big grin and say, "Smile, you're on *Candid Camera!*" There were streams of red dripping down every free wall space, piles of pasta everywhere, and all over the floor and the chairs and breakfast table, mountains of broken glass. Then I turned to the refrigerator, where I saw the door wide open and only a few inches of Pauillac's tail happily wagging away as if in a sirloin-induced frenzy. At the sound of my scream, Pauillac turned with the bloody-looking face of a morbidly obese hyena after a particularly vicious kill of an army of lesser jungle beings. Then it hit me. The broken glass. I immediately called the vet, with whom I was now on a first-name basis. I described the situation and my worry that Pauillac had ingested quite a bit of glass along with lasagna for ten. An experienced vet, he calmed me down and basically told me that if Pauillac survived the night and didn't start bleeding, she would probably be fine. This was exactly what happened. I ordered pizza for ten for dinner. And several more bottles of wine.

Shortly thereafter a friend came from Europe for a visit, and he came armed with several pounds of excellent Swiss chocolate for his chocoholic hostess. He had just arrived and put his enormous zippered duffel bag in the guest room and went to the kitchen with me for some coffee. After about an hour, when he told me about the chocolate he had brought, he went to the guest room to get the highly anticipated goods. He then calmly called me. I walked in and saw that Pauillac had unzipped his duffel bag, was lying down in it on top of the few clothes that remained in it, and had opened every bit of the chocolate and devoured it. Another panicked call to the vet—who was now number one on my speed dial—since chocolate is poisonous to dogs. Well, to *most* dogs. Pauillac was, again, just fine. It became quite clear that this animal had the gastro-intestinal constitution of a Sherman tank. However, I am still mad about missing out on all that fine European chocolate.

There were, of course, several instances of Pauillac getting so excited to see whatever what was on the other side of the sliding screen door that she could not be bothered to wait for anyone to open it. Instead, her canine cerebellum commanded her to charge *through* the screen door because it was simply in her way. Thus, the screen-door repair man was likewise high on my holiday list.

Then I decided that what Pauillac needed was some company. So one day, while driving by a Target store, I saw a sign for an animal adoption event. I turned the car around and took a look. There I saw a beautiful black-and-gray female terrier with dreamy eyes, exactly the same size as Pauillac, only this dog was calm as could be. They were canine equivalents of salt and pepper bookends. A furry Felix and Oscar. A dog partnership was born. She had the flattest back of any dog I had ever seen, and so I aptly named her Baguette, or Baggy for short. Unlike Pauillac, Baggy clearly had been loved and well taken care of and was well-trained. She assimilated into our household like white on rice and was truly a perfect animal, in all respects. While Pauillac would lick an intruding burglar to death, or alternatively give him the key to the household safe for even the slightest belly rub, Baggy was actually a great watch dog, barking just the right amount until she was sure the visitor was acceptable. She never did, however, get over her intense hatred for my kind-hearted, edge-clipping gardener, and would have taken out both of his ankles if given even half a chance. The gardener too made the top of the holiday list.

Perhaps the wildest Pauillac story occurred in mid-1996. Earlier that year I had gone on a trip to Mexico. On an impulsive whim, I purchased a beautiful and ornate wrought-iron bird cage. Not that I had any intention of ever getting an actual bird. I'd never even known anyone who ever had a bird. But the workmanship on the birdcage was intricate and interesting, and so I bought it. Once it was home, I didn't know what to do with it. So naturally I did what any red-blooded American would do; I bought not one bird, but two. Two of the messiest, noisiest, most obnoxious creatures on planet earth. And unemotional to boot—they never said a single word to me the whole time they lived with me, even though I fed and watered them and talked to them daily. But they sure were pretty to look at in that beautiful cage. After a few months, I was pretty sick of the morning screeching noises they made and the daily cleaning of their cage and surrounding floors. I never could figure out how they managed to throw their seed shells literally fifteen feet away from their cage. However, I learned that some mysteries in life simply are not to be solved or understood.

One afternoon, in June of 1996, when I was seven months pregnant and looking as though I had swallowed a twenty-pound watermelon, I realized I had forgotten to feed the birds that morning. And on my racing hormonal highway, I had forgotten to put Pauillac in the backyard while I did this. Pauillac used to sit under the cage, which hung from a chain from the ceiling, staring at those noisy creatures, and, I imagined, thinking of all of the terrible things she would do if only she were six feet tall. I opened the birdcage door to remove the seed tray, and the yellow bird flew straight out of the cage. Here I was, the size of Texas and running around the kitchen trying to catch a highly neurotic and now-panicked bird, when I saw Pauillac in the corner. I then realized what I had forgotten to do. The State of Texas did its level best, but I simply could not coax that bird back in the cage. Then the blasted bird took a nose dive literally right into Pauillac's wide open and salivating mouth. All that I could see was the final few inches of the bird's tail feathers. I tried to tackle Pauillac to get her to open her mouth, but given the girth of Texas, that failed. Then I did something that, despite all the havoc this dog had wrought over the years, I thought I would never live to do: I kicked Pauillac in the ribs. She was so startled that she opened her mouth, the bird flew out, I got it back in the cage, and I sat down and cried. Pauillac came up to me and licked my face. The next day the birds and the cage were gone, along with a lifetime supply of birdseed, given to a dog-less and cat-less secretary.

Pauillac and Baggy are now long gone, chasing birds and edge trimmers in dog heaven. And all dogs most certainly do go to dog heaven, accompanied by a large moving van carrying thousand-pound bags of T-bone steaks—or, in Pauillac's case, ten kilos of the finest chocolate that Swiss Francs can buy. All that remains are a handful of wild and crazy photographs and some even wilder and crazier memories. Now we have Demi

Moore and Ashton Kutcher look-alikes—a perfectly preserved though surgically unenhanced thirteen-year-old Dalmatian named Dottie, and a disheveled hairy five-year-old Bison Frisé boasting several names—Moose, Cesar, Latte, and, most recently Rerun—both of whom we rescued and both of whom provide more love and affection than ought to be legal. At least they aren't named after wine and bread.

Rescue a dog. Or two. Share your life and your love with them. Your life may never be the same, but you'll be so glad you did. And who knows, you may be the one who is really rescued.

11

Forgiving someone who has wronged you can be extremely hard to do. Not forgiving them is often far harder.

My parents divorced after a ten-year marriage in 1969 when I was eight years old. I never heard them raise their voices to one another or even have a significant argument, though I sensed even at that early age that my mother was deeply unhappy in their marriage. My father, I believe, would have stayed married to my mother for a lifetime. I saw my father exactly three times after the divorce, if you include the day I buried him.

Though handsome, charming and chivalrous, my father was a very troubled man. He never, I believe, fully recovered from his own sad and traumatic childhood experiences. Growing up in an elegant suburb of Vienna, Austria in the early 1930s with his parents and two older siblings, his early years were stable, pleasant and predictable.

My Austrian-born grandfather was studying in London when WWI broke out. He was summarily rounded up with other "enemy aliens," and spent several years as a prisoner, courtesy of the British, on the desolate Isle of Man. Since he spoke English and was a Swiss-trained master clock maker, he became indispensable as his captors perfected the timepieces for bombing capabilities. After WWI ended, he was released and returned to Austria, where became a well-respected diamond dealer and was highly sought for his abilities to repair towering (apropos for me) grandfather clocks of historical value. He had a very successful business. My grandmother originally hailed from the beer-producing town of Pilsen in the former Czechoslovakia. When she was an infant, her father died suddenly, and her mother remarried an older Viennese man with whom they moved to Baden, Austria. Family lore has it that my grandfather saw my eighteen-year-old grandmother walking by his store one day while he was outside smoking a cigarette, and then told his business partner that he would one day marry her. The partner laughed, so the story went, and said she was far too lovely a young lady for my grandfather, and that she would never have him for a husband. My grandparents were married exactly six weeks after that afternoon smoke—much to the chagrin, I imagine, of my grandfather's partner—and they were very happily married for over sixty years.

With WWII on the horizon and the Nazis descending upon Austria, my grandfather read the writing on the wall. He also didn't want to ever visit a prison again. Because my grandfather had means, was well-respected in both the Jewish and business communities, and was fairly well-connected, my grandparents were "asked" to leave their home, belongings and the family life they had known. My grandfather had managed to obtain forged and costly exit papers. A few days later, in the dead of night, my father, who was then twelve years old, together with his two older siblings and his parents, each carrying a small valise, left by train for Switzerland. Also with them was a box containing the fine work tools of my grandfather's trade; hidden carefully underneath those tools was the Torah from his rabbi father's synagogue. They ultimately made their way to Rotterdam, Holland where they obtained passage on a ship bound for New York. Along with thousands of other displaced and stateless persons with their own heartbreaking stories to tell, my father, his family and the old parchment Torah descended upon Ellis Island. Luckily, they had won lottery visas to enter the U.S. with the assistance of my grandmother's distant cousin who was then living in Warner Robbins, Georgia. The cousin was an elderly lawyer she had never met and who passed away not long after their arrival to the U.S. Like many people at the time, my grandfather's six siblings and their families refused to believe what was happening in Austria. Though urged by my grandfather to leave with them that night for Switzerland, they opted instead to remain in the only homeland they'd ever known. My grandfather never heard from any one of his six siblings or their families again, finding out after the war ended that every single one of them had perished in unimaginable ways in various concentration camps in Austria and Germany.

My grandfather was always a hard-working man, and immediately following their arrival he started rebuilding their lives in the small town of Macon, Georgia. He was kind and soft-spoken, with a twinkle in his eye and an ever-ready smile, though, to be sure, he was a very industrious and exacting businessman. At first he opened a small storefront jewelry and time-piece repair shop, and ultimately a much larger and even more successful one. Both were closed on Saturdays, the busiest shopping day of the week, in observance of the Jewish Sabbath. The adjustment to life in America was much harder on my grandmother, my father and his siblings, since they spoke no English at first and were used to living within a large circle of friends and family in an established community filled with art, music, culture, coffeehouses and fine restaurants. While beyond grateful to have been provided with safe harbor in the U.S. with their freedom and lives intact, they were fish out of water, as Macon was then a hot, dusty and segregated small southern town. Years later, when I was a teenager, my grandmother recalled for me the day of their arrival in Macon. She said that she elbowed my grandfather very strongly in the ribs as they got off the train from New York, admonishing him that he must have made a mistake and gotten them on the wrong train, because she was sure they had arrived in Africa. It was the first time she had ever seen anyone of African descent. When she began to fully grasp the black/white divide, she became convinced that they had arrived in Purgatory.

My grandmother, though not formally educated beyond high school, was nevertheless voraciously well-read, could name classical composers after a few notes of a symphony, was street-smart, and in some important respects, was far ahead of her era. In other arenas, she held on to her old-school ways, even when they didn't fit the time or the place. She was also an overbearing, tough-as-nails, Germanic-style, harsh, authoritative disciplinarian with my father. She could be both loving and generous, and brutal and harsh.

My father learned English, of course, and graduated high school, but he always felt like an outcast in the Deep South. And likely because of his war-time experiences, he was, as he described it, also physically allergic to religion in general and Judaism in particular. He rejected what was, in his opinion, his parents' archaic and strict religious ways. He took to eating vast amounts of pork and engaging in other acts of quiet rebellion, though always on the sly. Out of a twisted sense of respect, he would have first cut out his own tongue with a steak knife before he would have confessed these burning sentiments to either of his parents or his siblings. As he was unable to be honest with himself, he was thus unable to be honest with even those closest to him. Though he hated his parents' seeming dependence on the narrow confines of religion, he would never in a million years admit his decided and divisive defiance. Instead, he quietly seethed. He started to work with my grandfather, and while he had good, steady hands and was talented, he couldn't stand the work. He was conveniently drafted into the U.S. Army, which put his German language skills to work, but he had no stomach for military life or military authority. He bided his time, completed his military service, was honorably discharged, and couldn't wait to find a way to leave Georgia and seek his fortune elsewhere.

My father dutifully drove my grandmother once every four weeks for her monthly visit to the closest kosher butcher, which was eighty-five miles away in Atlanta. During one such trip in 1958, while crossing a busy intersection and carrying an armload of packages back to the car as his mother ran some other errands, my father literally bumped into an attractive and well-dressed woman. He promptly dropped all the meat packages in the middle of the street. My mother was working at the Israeli Consulate General nearby and had a few months earlier been transferred to Atlanta from the Israeli Consulate General in New York. Having rescued the meat from oncoming traffic, they chatted for a while on the corner, and then went for a cup of coffee. They discovered they had in common, among other things, an intense dislike for the Deep South, mainly due to the racial issues, as they were both die-hard liberals. A romance ultimately blossomed, and they decided to marry. My religious grandmother was utterly aghast that her youngest and favored son was going to marry a divorced woman. She neglected to notice at the time, apparently, that this woman was also well-educated, attractive, and employed by the Israeli government. She had also apparently and rather conveniently forgotten that her own step-father had married a widow with an infant. My grandmother was adamantly against my parent's union, made those feelings painfully clear every chance she got, and gave my mother no small amount of grief for several years thereafter, until one day she just stopped. My mother put in for a transfer out of Atlanta, and a week after their small wedding, they left Macon for good and drove west, where a position at the Israeli Consulate General's Office in Los Angeles awaited her. In the ensuing years, my father returned to Macon less than a handful of times, and my mother never returned.

Life took its course, and while my mother was overjoyed when she unexpectedly became pregnant with me, my father came to the realization, a bit too late, that he didn't want children—or, closer to reality, didn't really have a place for them in his troubled world. While my mother continued her work at the Consulate General, he held a series of jobs, and then opened a jewelry store which he stocked with jewelry purchased on credit. He sold his stock at a handsome profit, but unbeknownst to anyone else, intentionally neglected to repay his creditors. Several men in a big truck one day came and removed everything in our home not bolted down or built-in. I may never erase the memory of the look on my mother's face that evening when she returned from work to find an empty home. An unlikely and unexpected savior, my grandmother, stepped in from afar, paid off my father's creditors, and our furnishings and personal items were returned. My father's destructive behavior, however, continued unabated. Then, as my mother would years later tell me, it started to get really bad. He became more and more withdrawn, and then became increasingly and irrationally paranoid over the most innocuous things, people or events. And as is often the case in these situations, he thought nothing was wrong with him; it was everyone else who had a problem. When I was about four and starting to become naturally curious and mischievous, he started using fierce corporal punishment with me—usually with a leather belt, since that was handiest—as his only method of direct communication. When he started sleeping in their marital bedroom with a nine-inch butcher knife "secured" under his pillow, my mother realized there was no hope remaining in the situation, and understood, sadly, that her second marriage was over.

A few months after my father left our home, he picked me up one Sunday, and we spent the day at Disneyland. As we were leaving the amusement park, he bought me a stuffed Winnie the Pooh bear which sits now on a bookshelf in my teenaged daughter's bedroom. Over the ensuing years he called a couple of times, telling me he was working out-of-state, but wouldn't say what he was doing or precisely where he was. I once received a silver necklace with an Indian motif from New Mexico, and later a post card from somewhere in Colorado; never once a birthday card or a holiday call. After a while he became like a phantom in my mind as he traveled the southwest and elsewhere. I simply forgot about him and put him in an irrelevant place in my head and in my heart.

Two months following my mother's death in Hawaii, the only grandmother I had known, my father's mother, passed away. She and I had become very close after my parents' divorce, and I spent several summers with her in Macon. In a surprising familial twist, during those years, my grandmother ultimately became my mother's greatest champion, extolling her many virtues and her intelligence. Though she never directly uttered a disparaging word about my father to me, it was clear that she knew something was very, very wrong with him and that my mother did the right thing in divorcing him. After my grandmother died, I was overcome with a desire to find my father, and while I had no illusions that I would develop a meaningful or lasting relationship with him, I nevertheless wanted to attempt to make some sense of who was the man who, biologically at least, had been halfway responsible for my existence.

I learned from his older sister that he was again living in Southern California, and got his phone number. When I left Hawaii to begin my trek across the country to law school in Washington, D.C., I decided it was time to get in touch with him. I called him and he gave me his address. I arrived that afternoon at a small, dark, unkempt house, with all of the windows blacked out with aluminum foil. There he lived with three beastly sized German Shepherd barking machines, and a quiet, pleasant enough red-headed woman he vaguely introduced. There I sat for nearly two hours in the stifling summer heat without so much as the offer of a glass of water, and my heart pounding so loud I thought my ear drums would implode. I had come to learn what I could about this virtual stranger, and attempt to fill in my personal historical void. But he was simply unwilling to help, or in the clarity of hindsight, thoroughly incapable of doing so. Instead, he regaled me with irrelevant small talk. Mostly concerning his beloved dogs, the cases of his favorite chocolate he could now buy at the newly opened Costco nearby, and governmental attempts to restrict smoking in public places – he was a fanatical three-pack-a-day smoker. When I asked him if he had heard that my mother had died, he said he had and without skipping a half second of a beat, he immediately returned to a discussion of the high intelligence levels of those three blasted dogs. Clearly, it was time to leave.

Driving east across the country, I had plenty of time to think about this man, his early life, and the ever-present internal demons which destroyed his ability to lead a normal life and have even marginally honest discussions with me, his parents, or anyone else for that matter. I later learned that he had been married to the red-headed woman for over twenty years, but never told his parents because the woman was not Jewish. Here was a middle-aged man who was still was unable to tell his mother, my grandmother, who had mellowed considerably over the years, that he had, for whatever reason, chosen a different path. It became more and more clear to me during that long drive across America's heartland that asking or expecting him to be honest with me, when he was unable to be honest with himself, would be as effective as screaming at a person stuck in a car with a blown transmission to hurry up and get through an intersection when the light turned green. It just wasn't going to happen in this lifetime. I simply had to accept that part of my family of origin and try to forgive him, sad as it was, or otherwise let it eat me alive. As I pulled into Macon to visit the cemetery where my grandparents were buried, and placed the customary rocks on the top of their head stones, I chose the former. I somehow realized that not forgiving him would be holding on to the hope that I could truly recreate history. And that could simply not be done.

Twelve years later, while sitting in my office buried knee-deep in work, I received a frantic nine a.m. call from my father's older sister, an elderly woman still living in Georgia, to whom I was never close and whom I hadn't seen in nearly two decades. My father had died the night before, she told me, while with the three dogs in his garage, just six hours before he was scheduled to have open-heart surgery. She said the woman he lived with was about to have his body cremated. And would I, for God's sake, and the memory of my beloved grandparents, please see to it that he was properly laid to rest in a Jewish burial?

After I finished talking with my father's sister, I sat there for a few minutes, staring blindly at the telephone. I was six months pregnant at the time, and, as if on cue, my unborn child jolted me out of the many thoughts swirling in my head with a swift kick in the ribs. That child knew perhaps more than I did, for that kick went straight to my heart in a language I may never even begin to understand. That kick seemed to signal that if ever there were a time for complete forgiveness of the man who was my father but could never actually be or act like one, this was certainly it.

I called up an old friend whose extended family, I recalled, had a Jewish mortuary. They arranged for collection of my father's body from the morgue and would provide me with a rabbi for a short service. This gave me immediate pause as, although I knew very little about what made my father tick, I knew he had wanted zero to do with religion during life. He certainly would have wanted nothing to do with it at death. I spoke to the rabbi the mortuary provided in advance of the burial, and after I explained the situation, and my father's war-time past, he assured me the service would be "very neutral if that's what was wanted." And if I preferred, he would wear a dark suit instead of the traditional clergy robe.

A few days before the funeral, I called my father's wife and asked if I could pick up a suit for him. When I arrived, she handed me a large paper bag containing some old wrinkled clothes and his wallet. I asked whether there were any old family albums of my grandparents at their house. She said no. Knowing the answer in advance, I nevertheless then asked whether she had my father's ruby and diamond snake ring, a family heirloom he had worn for over thirty years and which my grandfather had made for him when he married my mother. She said no to that as well, though I was certain she was being dishonest with me about both things. When I left that house, I couldn't help but feel that, as the only child of my parents' union, the last vestige of my father's family memories were being unreasonably stolen from me. I tossed the paper bag into the trash can in the driveway and struggled to get my very pregnant body into my car. I then opened up my father's wallet. There were exactly four items in it, his driver's license, social security card, U.S. Army veteran's card, and a photo of me taken when I was about four years old. It was time to cry and to say good bye. For all that never was and would never be. The flood gates finally opened and cry I did. And with those many forgiving tears, real healing finally began.

At the funeral, there were three people present—the rabbi (wearing a dark suit), my husband, and I. My father's wife could not be bothered to attend. It was unbelievable to me, as she had been married to him, for better or for worse, for more than twenty years. But I had to let go of that as well. I simply had no room in my life then for any negativity or bad feelings, especially from a woman who truly had no meaning in my life. Besides, who knew what misery she had experienced or what resentments she harbored from two decades with my father? But still it was surprising. When the short service was over, my husband and I exited the memorial room into the hallway and were greeted by a somewhat frazzled, late-middle-aged couple who had obviously rushed to get to the brief funeral but missed it. I had no idea who they were. In an incredibly bizarre but somehow-fitting ending to very odd circumstances, the woman shook my hand vigorously several times, telling me that she was a very good friend of my mother's and had been for many years. I knew she was completely mistaken, chiefly because my mother had already been gone at that point for more than thirteen years. As this strange woman continued talking nervously a mile a minute, it became clear she had no idea who I was and was in fact referring to my father's second wife, a woman who never had any children.

Fifty-Fifty

My father was buried a few days later at a Veteran's Administration cemetery in the California countryside with the scent of the nearby orange fields in the air and an American flag draped over his coffin. The bronze plaque on his gravesite bears the date of his birth in Austria and the date of his death in the United States. And as a tribute to his parents, my loving grandparents, for whom religion was the paramount beacon guiding the ship of their lives, and to the very troubled son they loved, it also bears a small, but nevertheless distinct, Jewish star.

As wild a ride as I had with my father, both as a child and briefly as an adult, I know it could have been far worse. Not just factually, but emotionally. I know for a certainty that had I been unable to forgive him finally, I would likewise have been unable to reap the benefits of the many lessons I learned along the way. Most importantly, had I not forgiven him, I would have forever held onto the very worst parts of him—the anger, the denial and the damnation—instead of holding onto the good parts— his innate intelligence, his continuous desire to remake himself regardless of how misguided or misconstrued, and the fact that up until the very night he died, he kept in his wallet a faded photo of his four-year-old little girl. And that forgiveness led to compassion, which in turn led to empathy. Very often empathy, as hard as it may be to extend it to one who has wronged you, is the very best shield of self-protection and emotional preservation. Holding on to your own anger can do far more emotional long-term harm than anyone else's words or actions can ever do to you.

As the wheels of life rolled on, our healthy and beautiful little girl was born in the United States a couple of months later on August 7th, which happened to be the exact same day my mother had been born in Palestine, sixty-five years earlier. That wonderful woman our daughter would only know through the very rich fabric of my intricately woven personal memories. And the circle of life forgivingly and blessedly marched on without skipping a beat of the family drum.

12

Even if invisible at the time, there is some type of lesson in every situation.

My very first job was at the local McDonalds, a few blocks away from my home. After four heady capitalist days, I was summarily fired. Not for eating too much of the profits or forgetting to ask if a customer wanted fries with their order, but because I was only fourteen years old at the time. I had been hired by the stressed-out assistant manager on a Thursday, and he had forgotten to ask for my driver's license or state identification card. I worked over the weekend, thrilled with my new-found independence and the thought of a paycheck (though frankly I have never been able to look at French fries in the same lustful way since). When the manager returned to work on Monday, he apparently asked his assistant where my paperwork was, and when I couldn't produce it, was promptly shown the door.

As only a teenager can be, I was utterly devastated at the time. How would I save for a prom dress or a car? How would I explain to my much older friends why I got fired from such a lofty position at the Golden Arches? As it turned out, about a month later I got a better job at the same wage babysitting a younger child nearby while her mother worked. This had the added benefit of not requiring me to wear a dorky uniform or stand anywhere near hot, malodorous frying oil. I ultimately got both the prom dress and a beat-up old jalopy with a seriously cool eight track player! I thus was firmly planted in the teenage equivalent of über heaven.

Life went on, and then, of course, the lessons got exponentially more difficult. About a year later, my long-divorced mother met and fell in love with a seemingly nice man, who also happened to be from Israel and, like my mother, had been in the U.S. for many years. He was tall, good-looking, and charming with a ready smile, and he owned a travel agency. A few months later they made some loose plans to marry. I was happy for my mother, as she seemed happy, though I remained emotionally neutral regarding this man, mainly, I think, because he seemed fairly uninterested in having any real role in my life. I learned several months later that about six weeks after they got engaged, he had asked her for a large loan which he said he needed for his travel agency; apparently he had sold several hundred airline tickets on various carriers and had failed to pay for them. For reasons which I will never even begin to understand, my mother took a second mortgage out on our home and gave him a check for $50,000, a veritable king's ransom at the time. She never saw him again and was utterly devastated; it was, in fact, the only time I ever saw her cry. Then came the local police, the FBI agents, and the field investigators from the District Attorney's office. We learned that this creep had been under investigation for quite some time and had done the same thing to several women in several states. In fact, at the time this happened to my mother, this guy was simultaneously married to seven women that the authorities were aware of in as many states.

Although there was a long string of women who had filed complaints—and indeed some had been swindled of far more money than my mother had been—and despite the authorities' best efforts, this con eluded them. As far as I knew, he never paid for his crimes in any way. My mother never recovered any of the money she had "lent" him and also, I think, never fully recovered emotionally from the toll that awful experience took on her. From my perspective, it was utterly devastating watching someone I deeply loved go through that kind of heartbreak, betrayal and financial rip-off—perhaps even more so because the "loan" came from a place of kindness and hope for their collective future as a couple. This was a very emotionally draining experience I could certainly have lived without, especially at that impressionable age. The resulting negative lessons I gleaned from that experience—namely, an inherent fear and distrust anytime money got involved or disputed in a budding partnership of any sort—stayed with me for a long time and took me many, many moons to come to grips with. But come to grips I ultimately did.

I graduated from high school with the requisite amount of teenaged angst and distrust of authority. There was no way that I was going to be able to go straight to college. I thus took a year off and traveled around the U.S. mainland, stopping in cities long enough to earn money to continue onward. Because of the union work in hotels I had done in Hawaii, I was able in San Francisco to join the local AFL-CIO and obtained a coveted local union card. This allowed me to get contract work in the big chain hotels on a daily basis. The money was good and the shifts were usually only six hours in length, just long enough to feed a thousand people in a cavernous banquet room, serve them coffee and dessert, collect a check for the day's or evening's work, and leave. It was now nearly Christmas, and I had done this for a couple of months, I was making plans in my head to depart to British Columbia in a couple of weeks with a friend I had met during my travels.

A couple of days later, while working a luncheon banquet at the Sheraton Hotel on Market Street, a fight broke out in the kitchen between two middle-aged Eastern European men. One, I later learned was a Serb, and the other a Croat, harboring perhaps a centuries-old ancestral grievance, or perhaps one was just really pissed off that the other had cut in front of him in line to collect the next heavy tray of food. The shouting escalated, punches were thrown and the larger of the two men was literally sent airborne though the enormous kitchen and all 200-plus pounds of him landed on the back of my ankle.

The next thing I knew, I was spending the Christmas holiday week in traction at San Francisco General Hospital. This was a major drag, not just because I was basically alone in San Francisco, but also because it effectively cut off my income stream. Even though I was a union member, the contract nature of the job did not provide me with the ability to obtain unemployment or disability benefits. When I was about to be discharged from the hospital, a girl I had met a month before brought my old car to take me home. It was then I realized I wouldn't even be able to drive myself around to get groceries, as the old jalopy had a manual transition with a stubborn clutch and my left ankle now had a cast on it. Fortunately, I had a nice elderly woman as a downstairs neighbor who took pity on me and bought me provisions until my cast finally came off a couple of weeks later. She always bought a lot of prepared foods, something I wasn't used to, but grateful for nonetheless. Perhaps it was her way of hoping that I might stop hobbling loudly with my heavy cast on the hardwood floors of my sublet apartment in order to cook, since her apartment was directly below mine.

A couple of weeks later, still limping along, though now without a cast, I was invited to the home of the parents of my friend who had picked me up from the hospital. After dinner, her father, a very smart and affable principal at a local public high school, strongly suggested that I contact a friend of a friend of his who was a lawyer in the offices of Melvin Belli. In my youthful ignorance, I had no idea who Melvin Belli was, but if someone in his office could help me get some unemployment or disability benefits until I could go back to work, that was great. I made an appointment and went to their lavish offices a few days later. It was an impressive place, with beautiful furnishings and art, and it reeked of success. The lawyer I met with was youngish and pleasant, but quickly said unemployment or disability benefits were out of the question given the type of employment I had. Thinking our meeting was over, I got up to leave. But he quickly told me to sit down and asked me a few more questions about what transpired the day of the accident and during my hospital stay. He then had me sign a few papers and said he would make a few calls and get back to me.

About a week or so later the lawyer called me. By then I knew exactly who the notorious Melvin Belli was. Not just a wild and sometimes hugely unpredictable character with a similar style and often scandalous personal life, but a trail-blazing lawyer involved in often-newsworthy and highly lucrative cases. The young lawyer assigned to me said he had reviewed the hotel's accident reports and my medical records, and had contacted the airborne waiter's homeowner's insurance carrier. Apparently, the waiter had felt very badly about what had happened and had contacted his carrier on his own before I had ever heard of Melvin Belli's office. The matter was quickly settled. And a few days later, after signing some papers, I had in my hand a check for $3,000. All I had wanted was a few weeks of unemployment or disability benefits, probably at the time a few hundred dollars, and I ended up, thanks to this young lawyer, with more money than I had ever seen in my life. It was, at the time, nothing short of a monetary miracle. As I was probably overly effusive in the young lawyer's praise, he told me it really wasn't that much given that I had endured a significant fracture, spent a holiday week at a public hospital, was still limping and could not yet return to work. That was all true, but not to be dissuaded, I told the young attorney that he was the best lawyer in the entire world and then I promptly hung up.

I can't say with any degree of certainty that this experience alone was what prompted me to go to law school years later, but I can safely say that it made a great impression upon me. I saw that a lot of good could be done by lawyers when they had their hearts in the right place. I never did become a career litigator, much to the disappointment of my law firm mentors, mainly because I didn't want to have the type of unrelentingly stressful lifestyle they all seemed to have, but I certainly appreciated what the talented and dedicated ones were able to accomplish. It was a fairly odd lesson to have learned, given its Christmas Eve genesis in a large hotel's cavernous kitchen. But it was a valuable one nevertheless.

Thirty years later, while on a short trip to Israel, I was invited to a birthday party of a friend of a friend in a posh suburb of Tel-Aviv. While there, I went outside onto the large patio to get some air. One of the partygoers was smoking a cigarette, and we started chatting. He then instigated the requisite game of Jewish Geography—where questions are tossed out in rapid fire succession to see if there is any possible distant familial connection between you: Where do you live? Where are your parents from? Your grandparents? Were any relatives in the camps? Did they survive WWII? When did they arrive in Israel? And on and on and on. Enjoying the crisp night air, I played the geography game. All the while in my mind, I was willing to wager my significant year-end bonus that we were just two random strangers on a patio making small talk at a party.

The "geographical" connection I learned about that night was simultaneously so stunning and so utterly head spinning that it literally stole my breath away. The random coincidence of learning what I did and how I learned it also nearly caused me to keel over in shock. I had to immediately sit down on a nearby chair for fear that I would really pass out. This soft-spoken, educated, delightful sixty-year-old man was the son of the con who had swindled my mother a continent and a lifetime ago. And the son had perhaps even a sadder story still to tell about the louse that was his paternity, a man he hadn't seen or spoken to in over thirty-five years. I was promptly handed another glass of wine.

The son told me that the con had been married to his mother shortly before Israeli statehood occurred and had two children, himself and his younger sister. His parents were divorced when he was a young child, and his father had gone to Europe. The son later heard from extended family members that his father had then emigrated to the U.S. He quickly learned that any discussion or questions addressed to his mother about his father were taboo and totally off-limits. Growing up a fatherless son with all of his questions unanswered had left a deep void in this man's life. After he graduated from high school, he then served the obligatory three years of military service in the Israeli Defense Forces. By the time his military service was over, he was twenty-one years old and still possessed in him a burning, fatherless void, something I could certainly relate to. The son had managed to save nearly every penny of his meager military salary, then, together with his girlfriend, who had also just finished her mandatory military service, he bought tickets to New York to try to find his father and to see the U.S. So off they went to America with $5,000 to their names between them, stuffed in a money belt, hoping that would last for a lengthy trip across the country as they attempted to find his father.

They arrived in New York and stayed in a hostel for the first few days. After contacting some other Israelis in Manhattan with whom he had been put in touch by friends in Tel-Aviv, the son managed to obtain a phone number for his father in Queens. That night on the patio in Tel-Aviv, he described to me in vivid, heart-pounding detail, the feelings he had had decades before as he stood that sweltering afternoon in a public phone booth in Manhattan, calling the man who was his father and whom he hadn't seen or spoken to in over fifteen years. The father answered the phone and, according to the son, wasn't particularly surprised that the son had found him or made contact with him. After a brief conversation and hearing of their plans to tour the U.S, the son and his girlfriend were invited to the father's apartment for a visit. They returned to the hostel, showered and took the subway to the father's apartment in Queens.

On arrival that late afternoon, the son said, they were greeted warmly, and together they all had coffee and cake in the father's apartment. The son told me that he was "over the moon" at his father's seemingly generous manner and just at finally being in the same room with him and being able to start getting to know him. Hours later, the father suggested they go out for dinner. Before they left, the father told the son that the neighborhood was not a very safe one and they had a fairly long walk to his favorite restaurant, so if he had any cash on him, it should be put away for safekeeping. Without blinking an eye, the son gave the father the money belt containing all of his and his girlfriend's money, and they left for a restaurant several blocks away. After a long dinner and a few glasses of wine, the father paid the check and they all got up to leave. As they neared a subway entrance, the father suggested that since it was already so late and the apartment was ten blocks away, they should head back to the hostel to sleep. They then made plans to meet up for lunch the next day, since there was a good Israeli restaurant not far from the hostel at which the father wanted to eat. His father said he would bring the son's money belt with him then. The son and his girlfriend were tired, and didn't see the point in walking all the way back to the apartment since they would see him the next day, and so they agreed to meet him at the hostel at noon the following day. The father gave the son twenty dollars for subway tokens and breakfast and left. That was the last time the son saw his father, or the money belt.

At noon the next day, the son and his girlfriend dutifully waited outside the hostel. When one o'clock, then two o'clock came and went and the father didn't show up or answer the phone in his apartment, the son recounted to me that he "dove into a total penniless panic, though at that same time was simply unwilling to believe what had happened." It was, he described to me, as if his mother's silence over the years came loudly "crashing down on his head." That the truth was so outrageous, so painful to bear, so devoid of any semblance of morality, that she sought out silence as the only method she could muster in an attempt to protect him and his sister from the harsh reality that was their paternity.

At about three o'clock, the son and girlfriend took the subway back to the father's apartment on the slimmest of hopes that they were somehow wrong or mistaken as to where they were meeting. When they knocked on the door, it was opened partially with the door chain in place, and they were greeted suspiciously by an unfamiliar older woman. After they explained who they were, the woman removed the chain and opened the door. They were told by the woman that she had just returned from an extended trip to Florida and as a favor to someone else, had allowed the father to stay at her apartment while she was away and that he had looked after her cat. The father had left at nine o'clock that morning with his things and she had no idea where he went. The son knew then that that was the last of the father and the end of the dream of a cross country trip for which he and his girlfriend had saved for three long military years.

Panic again set in, made worse by the realization that they had only eleven dollars to their names and not even enough to pay their bill at the hostel. They returned to the hostel, then went to a pay phone and called a friend in Israel. The son briefly explained the situation and asked for a $200 loan to be wired to New York—he didn't dare call his mother.

After listening to the son's story, I was overwhelmed with deep sadness. At his loss, at my mother's, at mine, and for everyone else whose life this miserable con had entered and ruined or attempted to ruin. But my deepest sadness rested with the son. To have that kind of emotional and financial betrayal occur at the hands of one whose genes you share, who fathered you and who was supposed to teach you how to behave in the world and to protect you from its many ills—that was just unimaginable to me. And I could clearly see that it was, even so many years later, still psychologically crushing to him.

The son told me that night in Tel-Aviv that he had heard that his father ended up married to a wealthy woman in Florida. And seven years before, he had died there an old man. As I got up from my chair I said to the son, "Well, at least he can no longer do any more harm to anyone else." To which the son replied "*Baruch Hashem*"—thank God—and together we clinked our now-empty wine glasses.

That I had learned more of the truth about the con, thirty years later and nearly fifteen thousand miles away, by complete and total happenstance, was utterly mind-boggling. I had initially canceled that trip to Israel, then rescheduled it at the last minute. And that evening I had tried to beg off the party, since I was exhausted and didn't even know the birthday celebrant. But my friend insisted I go and reluctantly I joined the festivities. And then I ended up going outside and playing Jewish Geography with the one person out of the hundred people in attendance with whom I had an inextricable and nearly inexplicable connection. It is during moments like this in life when one really wonders about seeming coincidence and divine intervention. The lessons I learned from that awful experience, and the armor it made me wear subsequently for many years with those I didn't know well or fully trust, completely paled in comparison with the very heavy burden the con man's son and daughter had had to bear for a lifetime and would probably carry until the end of their days. As sad as all of this was, closing that circle gave me a sense of relief and of calm. The con was dead and gone and would do no more harm. To anyone. And learning that would simply have to be enough.

13

Often, the best, most positive thing you can do about other people's negativity or self-imposed misery is to get away from them.

We have all, at some point in our lives, had friends, lovers, colleagues or co-workers who were extremely negative in their outlook on life or seemed to live in a perpetual state of self-imposed misery or victimhood. To be sure, everyone has had their fair share, and some far more than their fair share, of trouble, heartache or just truly bad luck. The question in my mind has always been, what does one do with the bad things that sometime befall us? Often this question is more important than what has actually transpired. If you allow those bad things, perceived or real, to define you without attempting to see the lesson, and instead allow them to simmer and fester unexamined, then, as with a pot of boiling water, one runs the risk that ultimately the pot will empty out, dry up and eventually burn to kingdom come. The sad result is often a self-imposed victimhood caused by the perpetually overheated vat of misery.

For many years I lived with a man I'll call the Surgeon Who Wasn't. He was a highly trained, technically talented and financially successful surgeon. Patients often flew in from around the world to consult with him and then have surgery and he quickly climbed the ranks at a prestigious teaching hospital while his private practice flourished. The problem was that his motto was "A good patient is an unconscious one." The man simply hated his work; it was tolerable to him only when the

86

patients were sedated, unconscious and supine, and then only marginally.

Everybody has the occasional bad day or week at work where nothing seems to go right. Sometimes those bad days seem to go on for a very long time. Admittedly, lawyers by and large aren't the happiest bunch of people on earth, and law firms never come remotely close to resembling Disneyland. Dealing with the myriad of complex problems people and businesses can get into or find themselves in, and the ethical issues that sometimes arise, can often render it incredibly stressful work. I have certainly complained a fair amount myself over the last two-plus decades about various aspects of practicing—the long hours and accompanying stress, or some of the odd characters I've encountered in it. However, the Surgeon Who Wasn't was another breed altogether. His situation was perhaps even more complicated by the fact that he was extremely talented and paid very well for doing something he truly detested.

What the Surgeon Who Wasn't had really wanted to do since the time he started college was to go into his step-father's hugely successful retail business. There were, however, two older step-brothers already in the business and the step-father didn't see the need for a third. The step-father also firmly believed, after living with his step-son for ten years, that he didn't possess the requisite business acumen or the temperament for a career in retail. So instead, the step-father steered him toward medical school and sweetened the deal by picking up the entire tab. While for many people the opportunity to get an all expense paid trip to medical school would be considered manna from heaven, in his case, it was the commencement of his descent into the darkness of victimhood. As he hadn't really planned to go to medical school, he didn't have the grades to get admitted to one in the U.S. So he spent the first two years of medical school in Mexico, and then transferred to a good school in the Midwest, followed by an internship, residency, and specialization at highly prestigious hospitals.

The Surgeon Who Wasn't played the game, but was miserable every single day and every step of the way. He was able during working hours to maintain the façade of the good Dr. Marcus Welby. But the mask he wore was torn off with a vengeance somewhere between the operating room theater and our front door. At first, I thought it would pass. But a bad few months turned into a bad few years, which turned into just a consistently bad and negative existence. His misery followed him like a continuous shadow everywhere he went and seeped into everything he did. It so invaded his personal existence that after a while, nothing gave him any real pleasure in life. As is often the case with depression, the dark shadow then commenced a pleasure theft from those around him, myself included. Because he was so miserable and couldn't see a way out—even though, of course, there were plenty of exit avenues—it seemed that he wanted company to share in his misery. He therefore fed me a steady diet of humiliation from the misery-loves-company cook book. Friends fell away and couldn't understand why I stayed with him. Frankly, I wasn't too sure myself at the time, other than I was doing it out of a vague sense of not wanting to fail at something that I had put my heart into, especially given the amount of time I had invested in the relationship. After so many years together, it was very difficult to pull the plug, even though many of those years were very unhappy and the memories of good times had completely faded. It often seemed as though I was just about pulling a ligament, several in fact, in my attempts to create a positive atmosphere in my life with him, while at the same time trying to stay true to myself and the way I wanted to live. It was, ultimately, a completely impossible task.

The Surgeon Who Wasn't refused any help. Doctors often don't seek medical or psychological intervention when they need it. Instead they tend to prolifically self-medicate. Finally, the Surgeon Who Wasn't had a nervous breakdown following a dramatic and fictitious crisis he created at a nearby hospital. Shortly after that he stopped practicing medicine altogether.

As hard as his crash and the aftermath were to deal with, in a way I thought they were good things, in that perhaps this would cause him to finally get some help and get his life on track. For three more very long years I stayed with him, watching him do virtually nothing. When it became clear that he would never return to any work at all in any form, or even seek help to guide him, I finally left. The Surgeon Who Wasn't never did return to any kind of employment and remains alone. Such an incredibly sad waste of high intellect, and so many years of education, training and talent.

Years later I came to the understanding that the Surgeon Who Wasn't and my father shared some characteristics. And although they were two very different men with vastly different backgrounds, ethnicities, religions, upbringings and opportunities, I realized rather shockingly that there were some very distinct threads of psychological similarity. Both were very smart and capable, but internally miserable people who viewed the world through their lenses of self-imposed victimhood. Both were men who would not or could not, for completely different underlying reasons, tap into internal or external sources to aid in their understanding or their healing in order to become productive or successful or to maintain a modicum of productivity or success, in either their professional lives or their personal ones. When this vague sense of repetitive history finally materialized in my admittedly stubborn brain, it literally frightened me into a clear focus. It also forced me, brick by brick, to dismantle the way I viewed my role in a romantic relationship and to rebuild my role in such a way that I wouldn't be destroyed along the way to keeping peace at home.

I was lucky in that I was able to leave and begin anew. And of course things are often much clearer in hindsight. Looking back, I find it incredible that the similarities between these two men, which were psychologically very significant, didn't set off an ear-splitting alarm in my head from the get-go. Or at least after a year or two. But there were probably two things at play here. One was what I call the "packaging differential." These two men on the outside were so different that the concept never even entered my head. As well, I believe that I had to experience this as an adult in order to make sense of parts of my childhood experience with my father which had gone unresolved for so long. As an adult I was able to make certain choices; and in this case the choice was to leave. Resolution would have to come from within. From within it came, and leaving was most definitely the right decision.

This got me thinking about choices in general, and reminded me of what the late Dana Reeves once said. Ms. Reeves was a spirited and amazing woman, a Superwoman, really, in her own right. She was also wife to the real Superman, the late Christopher Reeves. The Reeves family had suffered unspeakable tragedy—first with his horrible horseback riding accident in 1995, resulting in a spinal cord injury, paralysis and ultimately his death; then Ms. Reeves' own illness and untimely passing at the age of forty-four in 2006. When she was taking care of her husband and young son with remarkable bravery and fortitude before she fell ill, Ms. Reeves so aptly said, "Some of the choices in life will choose you. How you face these choices, the turns in the road, with what kind of attitude more than the choices themselves, is what will define the context of your life." Those wise words really struck me as gospel truth. Your attitude about those choices in life, whether they were chosen for you or by you, will permeate your existence and become an integral part of it. It will also define the path you take, wherever it leads to, and will determine how you fare and, ultimately, the kind of person you evolve into.

Victimhood and self-imposed misery are not gender-specific, nor are they reserved for those of any particular background or age group. There are those, for example, who complain incessantly about a bad marriage. I'm not talking about discussions surrounding the occasional disagreements or spats, or the day-to-day issues that arise when two people try to live under one roof or raise children together. I'm referring to those people who have had spouses do some really awful things that either didn't get resolved or were, in their eyes, resolved wholly unsatisfactorily. We'll call these people the Bickersons.

For a long time I had such a friend. I had known her for many years and we were very close, both expatriates living in France at the same time, sharing, among other things, a somewhat similar international background and education. She had a boyfriend of a few years who, while charming, smart and very successful, was also an incredibly self-absorbed, arrogant, and racist man. She married him around the same time I got married, and also had her first child about the same time I had mine. We remained very close over the years, despite the different countries we both ultimately moved to and in which we put down roots. We spoke several times a month, often for hours at a time, and saw each other a few times a year in various cities. And after the kids came along, we would drag them along on our visits. After a period of time, several friends from our original circle, myself included, stopped visiting her when her husband was around, as we became unable to bear both his arrogance and his increasingly raging racism, both of which, just like stinking rotten eggs, seemed to get worse with age. When my friend was seven months pregnant with her second child, she learned that her husband had been regularly visiting local brothels in the city where they lived and actually keeping several women gainfully in his nocturnal employ.

Learning this was, understandably, nearly unbearable for her to tolerate much less try to comprehend. And no doubt it was made worse by the late stage of her second pregnancy. She was devastated. Her friends rallied around her with unwavering support for whatever path she decided to take. She had a graduate degree and was capable of earning a substantial income. And she certainly had more than enough means to support herself and her children if she decided to leave the situation. She ultimately decided to remain in the marriage when her husband vaguely intimated that he would cease his extracurricular activities though he never attempted to resolve the underlying issues—assuming they were in fact able to be resolved. As it turned out, my friend's husband did not change his behavior, he just occasionally became a bit more discreet about it.

The lengthy phone calls and visits with my old friend over the ensuing years got harder and harder to tolerate. Not because of the problems she faced, which were admittedly enormous and heart-wrenching, but because she chose neither to do anything about them, nor to alter her expectations in such a way so that she could live in peace with the path she chose. The Bickersons fought incessantly about everything under the sun, very important things and highly irrelevant ones—from soup to nuts, and everything imaginable in-between. The calls would go on for hours, with rabid complaints about her husband's various recent offensive activities and his many, many shortcomings. Like all of us mere mortals, Mrs. Bickerson was of course far from perfect herself, but she was an old and dear friend and I loved her like a sister. Following a particularly lengthy and venomous phone call about two years later, I noticed that the call made me feel so grimy and so awful that I felt I needed to go to a car wash in a convertible in order to wash off the bad feelings I had. I could no longer listen to her long-winded victim diatribes as she remained in a situation intolerable to her and without altering anything about her world. At first I tried to steer our conversations to more neutral territory, such as our children or careers. But she needed to be able to communicate freely and continuously her never-ending marital high-drama nightmare.

I then spoke to a mutual friend who lived near the Bickersons and who had likewise avoided Mr. Bickerson completely. Early one evening the friend—who is of African descent—was visiting Mrs. Bickerson at her house when Mr. Bickerson arrived home a bit early. Against her better judgment, but in an effort to be diplomatic, she agreed to stay for a glass of wine. Mr. Bickerson must have gotten a severe case of quick-onset amnesia and temporarily lost his mind, as he went on one of his hideous racist rants, like a squeaky hinge well-oiled by a second bottle of wine. Without saying a word, our mutual friend put down her glass and left. This woman had disengaged from all but the most routine and superficial conversations with Mrs. Bickerson and never again went to her home. The mutual friend said to me, "For your own mental health, sometimes you just have to do what you have to do, and sometimes that includes a one-way ticket to Splitsville." Wise words.

I tried the neutral-topic drill for a few more months, but it felt neither true nor satisfying for me and neither, I imagine, neither did it for Mrs. Bickerson. Slowly, over the ensuing months, our relationship and that of our children simply faded away. It made me very, very sad, and years later I still miss my smart, lively and vivacious friend. However, I could no longer keep her company in the toxic cauldron she chose to stir constantly, nor was I willing to join her caustic and self-imposed cursed crusade of victimhood. While allowing this to fade away was difficult, I ultimately felt that it was the right thing to do. Not just for my own emotional preservation, but because I also knew intuitively that I couldn't possibly help her, as help wasn't what she was seeking. All of that said, it was tough, and my heart still aches for Mrs. Bickerson.

For better of for worse, you are stuck with your family of origin and some of the stories, legend and lore that go with its constituent parts. They become part and parcel of who you become, both the positive and the negative. However, I finally learned that I did not have to adopt those stories as my own. Once you grow up, literally and figuratively, you do not have to twist yourself into a pretzel in order to try and make a miserable person happy. It cannot be done in any event, no matter how hard you try and despite your very best-intentioned efforts. This is one arena where success is simply impossible. The hardest thing to grasp in these situations is to know when it's time to throw the proverbial towel in the ring. Sometimes it's in the first round after a broken and bloody nose, and sometimes it's in the ninth with a sense of two black eyes, a split lip and double vision. Sooner or later though, the bell will clang loud and your most personal referee will call the bout, thus saving you from near-terminal concussive mind torture so that you too do not join the miserable ranks of the self-imposed victim. And after you return to the locker room of your life, shower off the sweat, wipe off the blood and dress the wounds you endured, you will be so glad you didn't. It's a membership in a very exclusive club that you absolutely do not want to join.

14

Eat good food. Your body and perhaps your mind will thank you.

This chapter heading seems so simple, it sounded kind of lame to me as I typed it. Who, after all, would eat bad food if given a choice? All one has to do is take a look around at the ever-increasing girth of many in Western societies—and in the last twenty years, some Eastern ones as well—to see that the sad fact is that many people will willingly eat badly. Because of my ethnic background and the role eating plays in our cultural arena, the kitchen in general and food in particular hold a revered place in my universe. While my kids would say I'm not the best nor the worst cook in the world, my husband, bless him, will eat anything placed in front of him which doesn't in any way contain the color green. The fact that he is so easy to feed however, has relatively little to do with my cooking skills and far more to do with the fact that he is a self-contained, one-man fire hazard in anything even remotely resembling a kitchen. In fact, rumor has it that he is on the very top of the County Fire Department's emergency watch list. Just a few months ago he opened the refrigerator, took out some leftover pasta covered in tin foil, and placed it in the microwave. From across the kitchen, I watched him shut the door and start punching buttons. No mortal has ever seen me leap so fast as I did in that kitchen before he could tap the start button on the microwave—except, as I mentioned earlier, when my own canine version of Marley nearly swallowed my pathetic parakeet whole. And no one ever will.

Eating is also one of the greatest pleasures of traveling. In fact, even when I was traveling as a "starving" student on a budget now reminiscent of laundry change, and souvenir or other shopping was out of the question, eating remained the ultimate thrice daily indulgence whether it was a crunchy baguette and some creamy brie from a Paris marché, a bowl of steaming udon from a Tokyo soup stall, or some hot falafel from an Arab kasbah stand. The food was part and parcel of the travel experience, but the travel experience was likewise part and parcel of the culinary experience. An inextricably intertwined convergence of what are, for me, two distinct though necessarily combined cultural events.

Eating a meal in the omnipresent food halls of Singapore with its mélange of Chinese, Indian and Malay influences is utterly transcendent insofar as eating incredible food on concrete tables in ninety degree heat with ninety percent humidity can be transformative. But I did notice on my last day there during a recent trip that in one of my favorite food halls, there was, mysteriously (and frankly, rather obviously out of place), a Mexican food stall as well. While I truly love Mexican food, the cultural and geographical disconnect while melting in the South Asian summer heat and humidity simply precluded me from even thinking about crunching on a taco. At least not without the benefit the cold clarity of an accompanying ice-blended frozen margarita could provide.

The Singaporean-Mexican food-stall disconnect reminded me of a Sunday evening in Tel-Aviv several years back. As Jerry Seinfeld seemed to make clear during American prime-time television, and then forever after during all hours in reruns, Jews the world over eat Chinese food on Sundays. Apparently it is no different in Israel. So not to make a liar out of Seinfeld, I went on a Sunday with an Israeli friend to a Chinese restaurant not far from Hayarkon Street near a popular beach in central Tel-Aviv. It was a family-run restaurant, and by that I mean an extended Chinese family. We were seated and given menus containing culinary choices in four languages—Hebrew, Arabic, English and Chinese. Why I was surprised by what transpired I still don't know. The Chinese waiter, who looked to be in his early thirties, came to our table to take our order. While I certainly speak enough Hebrew to order any kind of dinner—though I can't read a single word of Hebrew—for some reason I ordered in English, but I noticed the waiter wasn't writing anything down. *What a memory he has,* I remember thinking at the time. My friend ordered in Hebrew, then told me he didn't think the waiter spoke English. Then the Chinese waiter looked at me expectantly and asked me in perfect, flawlessly fluent though accented Hebrew, whether I wanted white or fried rice or noodles. He then asked me in Hebrew what I wanted as a main course. I was somewhat flabbergasted. It was, for me, a complete ethno-cultural inversion to see this Chinese man, just a few years older than I was then, speak so comfortably in the native tongue of my Israeli-French mother. Honestly, though, in the clarity of what is sometimes 20/20 hindsight—or in my case now, 50/50 hindsight—it could not have been any more bizarre than it was for the locals when I first arrived in Northern Japan in the early 1980s speaking grammatically correct, though heavily accented, Japanese. To put this into proper cultural context, one must delve a bit further into my own past.

The house I grew up in was a linguistic bowl of international, finely-mixed chopped suey. My mother was born in Old Yaffo, a port town in Palestine, in 1931, and grew up speaking Hebrew, French, German, Yiddish and English. She came to the U.S. with her work in 1954 and then learned Spanish. My father, born in 1927 in Baden, Austria, spoke German, Czech, Yiddish and Polish and came to the U.S. in 1938 as a teenager and learned English. They married in 1959 and our household was fairly typical of the times—absolute assimilation to American life and culture, with the English language of paramount importance. Thus my father decreed that only English would be spoken at home, although he was never able to completely lose his own accent. While I certainly now understand his reasoning – perhaps stemming from an almost nationalistic neurosis—I still think it was a linguistic and cultural mistake. The ability to think and communicate clearly in another language does not, in my opinion, make one culturally or socially isolated; in fact, I think it makes you much more able to understand the culture you live in. And I believe it also provides a far broader context within which to observe and traverse it. However, given my mother's line of work in the Israeli Foreign Service, and the wide linguistic variety of the international cast of characters that often found themselves at our home often at odd hours, my father's edict was a difficult one to uphold. As a method of survival, coupled with a child's curiosity as to what was going on, I nevertheless picked up enough in several languages to make myself understood, and certainly, at least, to order food in a restaurant. However, because of my father's household rule much of this had to be done in a clandestine manner, and I wasn't permitted to speak to my mother in her native tongue, at least while my father was at home. It therefore became a continuous, rabid game of linguistic and cultural Olympic speed-style ping pong, traversing back and forth to Anglo-American culture from whichever one was the one du jour. I never did learn to read the Hebrew alphabet, due to simple laziness. I am really fluent and comfortable now in only two languages, passable in a third, with the balance at the skill level that I call "enjoyable-travel capable." And as a result, I am irrationally jealous of those people who are able to read and write fluently in several languages, and to speak with their parents in their native tongue with ease, comfort and clarity. When I discussed this topic with a favorite Israeli uncle who speaks half-a-dozen languages rather well himself, he quipped with a twinkle in his one good eye that it was all chatterbox nonsense, since "Everyone alive knows that there are only two real ways to learn a foreign language with any degree of technical precision. One is in prison, and the other is in bed." Okay then. And while he's perhaps right, I'll stick to the latter thank you.

Fifty-Fifty

So now, facing a Chinese restaurant owner in Tel-Aviv who not only spoke flawless Hebrew but undoubtedly could read it as well would have silenced me and made me green with envy had I not been so bloody hungry. I mumbled something about Kung Pao chicken and white rice and off he went into the kitchen—unkosher, of course, as pork was, thankfully for my dinner partner, squarely on the menu. My dinner companion and I thus spent most of the evening talking about migration, culture, language, and possible opportunities lost and potentially gained as a result. He said that while this Chinese restaurant was successful, and the food was in fact very, very good, he felt rather sad for the Chinese proprietor and his family. The proprietor's children were Israeli-born, went to Israeli public schools, and by all accounts were Israeli through-and-through, though of course not Jewish, at least not ethnically Jewish. Thus my Israeli dinner companion worried, that even though the Chinese restaurant owner and his family were fluent in Hebrew and his children socialized and schooled in Israel, what the future would hold for this Chinese man's children? Whom would they marry? How would the proprietor's family and others in the same situation ultimately adjust to possible full assimilation in the Jewish state?

This conversation brought home to me once again the modern yet age-old immigrant question, brought about by an older generation seeking a better life outside their ancestral homeland. As I pondered this cultural-generational question, I also noted the culinary juxtaposition of eating a juicy, sweet, local Jaffa orange, while at the same time sipping pungent, boiling-hot Chinese tea. The proprietor's kids, I thought, would find their way, as most children of immigrants ultimately do, though not devoid of the requisite amount of identity confusion and cultural angst. They usually do this either by further assimilation right where they are, and adopting, adapting and maintaining a mélange of local traits, customs and rituals mixed in with their own; or by returning to their ancestral homeland to

99

seek companionship and family ties with ones who perhaps hold a cultural familiarity and identity closer to that of their parents.

As the offspring of immigrants to America, I can say with absolute certainty that this is not by any means a smooth transition. As immigrants' children traverse young adulthood, they often struggle with simultaneous feelings of swimming upstream against a cultural identity crisis and being beached by desires to assimilate fully. And of course, there is unfortunately, no "one size fits all" path to figuring this out and solving the inherent dilemmas these issues present. About all that is certain in the confusing cultural conundrum experienced by immigrants' children is that they must grasp and come to grips with the fact that they neither fully belong to their parents' culture, nor do they fully belong to the culture in which they were born and raised. Only in this way can the cross-cultural and generational divide be embraced and then accepted, irrespective of how the mixed amalgam ultimately looks.

My head was still spinning from swimming deeply in the pool of this personally pertinent topic when it came to me just how important a role food plays in the social experiment that immigrants experience as part of assimilating into a new country; as well their impact on the society of the country they have adopted. And indeed, in a country as small as Israel the impact is probably much more tangible than in one the size of the U.S. So ended my culturally confusing experience at the Israeli/ Chinese restaurant as I had to meet a cousin nearby for a late night dessert and the drink that accompanies all social discourse in Israel – the mandatory cup or two or five of coffee. Besides, I was already twelve hours and one succulent meal ahead, thinking with a satiated stomach about what tomorrow would bring at the home of my aunt—a hearty Israeli breakfast of strong European coffee, a wide variety of creamy white cheeses, pungent, tangy green and black olives, warm breads, and the requisite finely chopped salad of juicy, blood-red tomatoes and fresh, crunchy cucumbers. Good food once again serving as the almighty and revered captain on my ship of international explorations: gastronomic, intellectual and emotional.

Good food and a good meal of course mean different things to different people. But no matter how you view the dining experience, what you eat, along with the Russian roulette mixture of your personal DNA, will affect how long you live and how healthy you remain. All I suggest is that the food which gives you sustenance be remotely good in the sense that its contents can actually be pronounced by the average teenager—at least most of the time anyway. I have been known to eat—all by myself on occasion—an entire bag of extra crunchy Cheetos with a Diet Coke chaser and a large bag of peanut M&M's while watching an utterly mindless movie, and thoroughly enjoying every single bite. Admittedly though, this usually happened just after final exams in college or grad school. And meals should be eaten in the company of a good book, a good view or interesting companions or loved ones. The old cliché says, "We can eat to live or live to eat." Frankly, I think we can do both and glean a great deal of pleasure along the culinary way not to mention some interesting cultural insight. However you do it, every good meal most certainly should be enjoyed and revered—preferably with a good glass of wine—as if it were your last.

15

Sometimes making a difficult decision leads one to take the path of least resistance. The decision may ultimately not be the right one, but it may serve an important purpose in the grand scheme of things.

Several months prior to graduation from law school in Washington, D.C., I fortunately had three job offers from which to choose. I was still grappling with where to go and what to do. Despite law school's rigorous and intense theoretical study, it doesn't really prepare you for the day-to-day reality of life as a practicing attorney. Thus, I had a lot of difficulty making a decision. Each job offer was in a different city, and offered a different type of practice. One was with a mid-sized well-known litigation firm in Seattle at a high salary, and the second was with an international bank in Washington, D.C. at a mid-level salary. The final offer was with a smaller boutique Honolulu firm where I had spent the summer following my second year of law school clerking under the watchful eye of a very talented and kind-hearted lawyer, at a relatively low salary. When the deadline came for the final decision, I still had not reached one. The clock was quickly ticking and I was up against a wall. I ultimately took the path of least resistance and accepted the position in Honolulu, both because it was familiar and I enjoyed working with the partner who made me the offer. It was certainly not the worst possible decision I could have made under the circumstances, but as it turned out, it was not the right one for me at the time.

Not long after I accepted the Honolulu job, the group within that firm that I worked with and was to join upon graduation merged with a much larger, more politically connected firm. I was, as the partner who had hired me happily told me in the phone call, "part of the merger package." I was grateful I had been "merged," as I had already rejected the other two offers, and so I decided to go with the newly merged flow.

I graduated from law school and moved back to Honolulu. I then spent the better part of that summer studying hard for the Bar exam while house-sitting for my beloved college history professor. My main responsibility, other than studying, was to feed her nineteen-year-old cat while she and her art professor husband went to Europe on a research trip. It was also then that I started praying on a daily basis that the ancient arthritic feline would live until their return. I sat for the four-day-long Bar exam in July, then immediately took off for a planned trip to Switzerland. While away, I received word that the Bar results would be posted on an exterior window at the Hawaii Supreme Court the night of my return. I arrived at Honolulu at one thirty in the morning after a truly terrible flight, and a good friend picked me up at the airport. We drove directly to the Supreme Court, and found the window with the list taped on it. The only problem was that the list had the names printed alphabetically in two columns left to right instead of up and down, and so I missed my name. Crestfallen, I thought I failed, and stopped looking at the list. My friend refused to believe I didn't pass, and in fact was the one who continued looking and found my name. Then we both started screaming. Very loudly. So loud apparently, that some man on the street randomly appeared out of nowhere and asked if we were okay. I was more than okay. I had reached the finish line. Or as I would later learn, the starting line.

My first day as a practicing attorney was total chaos and complete pandemonium. It was none other than the infamous Black Monday, October 19, 1987. Most of the firm's clients were businesses. With the six-hour time difference to the

East coast, by the time everyone woke up in Honolulu and got to their respective offices, many of the firm's clients were already in severe financial pain.

Following the merger with the larger firm, the old firm's make up and client base had changed considerably, and I found myself doing all kinds of work in which I had zero interest, and often found myself in court at the last-minute arguing a case on a senior partner's behalf because he had a last-minute schedule conflict. As I was the lowest person on the firm's legal totem pole—or maybe just because I happened to be present when the need arose—I was nominated with military-style precision. And I often found myself reading the lengthy case file as I walked the three blocks to the courthouse. It wasn't what I had thought I would be doing, and I wasn't getting the kind of work experience I wanted to obtain.

It was about this time that I also came to the realization that although my heart was in the right place, I had probably returned to the islands for the wrong reasons. While I truly loved the beautiful islands, the gentleness of its people and its climatic, rhythmic way of life, I had thought that returning there after law school would provide me with some semblance of home—the sense of home I had missed terribly during the three long and freezing years I spent in Washington, D.C. But my mother was gone, along with the two sets of neighbors who had adopted me following her death. Also, many of my college friends and my three college roommates to whom I remained close were then living in different parts of the world. As a result, the islands no longer provided me with the comforting womb it had in years past. So after a couple of years, I felt it was time to move both firm and city. So when headhunters started to ring my office to sniff out potential interest, I started accepting their calls.

Looking back, from a purely professional standpoint, it probably would have been wiser to have taken the position with the international bank that I was offered, and braved a few more cold winters on the East coast. But of course second-guessing a decision, and twenty-five years later at that, is truly an exercise in futility. Besides, I can never now know what that position would have really been like on a real, day-to-day basis, nor could I possibly know what that would have ultimately meant in the trajectory of my life, professionally or personally. All of that said, while my decision to return to Honolulu may not have been the very best one for me at the time, it did serve to formulate more clearly in my mind the kind of work I did and didn't want to do going forward. It also, of course, more clearly brought home to me the age-old concept that indeed, you can never really go home again. Both of these things were important to grasp. And understanding them led to some better, more thoughtful decisions. Though of course, inevitably, sailing isn't always smooth in the sea of life, and there were certainly some more missteps along the way. But in the grand scheme of things, learning these things at that stage allowed me to move on in order to reach the next stage in my life—and, of course, to learn the next important lesson.

16

Being around those who suck the air out of a room will ultimately leave you short of breath—or worse, literally gasping for air.

Everyone knows the type. The outwardly successful person, smart, boisterous, charming, moves ten miles a minute, knows a billion stories about a million different things and is only too happy to share them with any adoring or available audience. The intrinsically Type-A kind of high-intensity, high-octane, usually highly controlling, manic person. This is not to be in any way disparaging of Type-A people in general, especially since my terrific husband is a solid Type-A and I happen to be a happily recovering, or at least slowing-down, Type-A person – Hi, my name is Julie and I have been Type-A free for twenty-six days.... Indeed, I'm sure the reason so much gets done in the world is because of a vast proliferation of Type-A people, especially in the U.S. Perhaps it's something in the milk. You want to get something done right away? Give it to your nearest Type-A colleague, friend, acquaintance or offspring. But don't forget the mirror—the nearest Type-A person may perhaps be lurking right there in its shining reflection.

Perhaps because of my own general Type-A-ness, I have often found that I gravitated toward Type-A people in general and, unfortunately, the Type-A high-intensity manic control freaks in particular. When I was younger, far more naïve and even less aware of the havoc these types of characters could wreak and the collateral damage which could ensue, I was often like a moth to the control freak's shining manic flame.

Once I made the initial difficult decision to leave Honolulu, the rest came in rather quick succession. While I was pondering an offer I received from the London office of a large, well-known British firm for a position on its aviation finance team, another headhunter called me with a position in the Los Angeles office of a large Wall Street firm. The busy partner there was looking for a transactional associate, and had a huge book of East Asian business, most of which was Japan related. He wanted someone culturally comfortable with the Japanese people and familiar with the language. This sounded right up my alley and, as it was a New York firm, had the very seductive attraction of a New York-based salary. The annual salary was more money than both of my parents combined had ever in their lives earned in a year. I flew out a week or so later over a long holiday weekend to meet the hiring partner and discuss the position.

The thirty-six-year-old hiring partner was a short, rotund, balding man, and what remained of his hair was already prematurely snow-white. He had a ready, broad smile and a nearly continuous barrage of witty one-liners. He was clearly very smart, had a lot of interesting work, and I thought I would learn plenty of sophisticated technical skills from him. We did the interview and geographical dance for about half an hour in his expansive and lavishly decorated 16th floor office. I spoke of my disappointment that my current firm had merged shortly after I had accepted their offer, which quite changed the nature of the firm and the practice. Then without a warning, he jumped up from his chair as if it were on fire and said, "I'm starving, I need a corned-beef-and-rye. I know a great deli, let's go." And off we went to a west-side deli in his decked-out, late-model, black Porsche. We ate a veritable mountain of greasy corned beef, with cole slaw dripping in artery-clogging mayonnaise, and drank a gallon of iced tea. On the way back to the office, he asked if there was anyone I wanted to call from his newly-installed car phone. Though I was dying to try the boxy, magical apparatus, I politely declined. He then called the human resources department of the firm and told whoever answered that he "had just hired his newest right hand WO-PERSON," instead of "woman"—lest, I suppose, my first name could be considered a man's name in some strange HR universe.

Admittedly, while I knew this man was super smart, I knew even then that he was a slightly odd bird. But I had no idea, nor could I have then even begun to imagine just how odd he was. I flew back to Honolulu and gave notice to the kind-hearted partner who had originally hired me, and got his blessing. I then made plans to leave my beloved islands for another new adventure.

I arrived in L.A., found a tiny apartment not too far from the beach, and started working a few days later. The firm was welcoming, the work was interesting, and after two months, it was time to take three weeks off to cram for yet another Bar exam, this time the notoriously difficult California Bar exam—the one with a dreaded and well-publicized sixty percent fail rate. The afternoon on my last day before I left to study, the managing partner of the firm waltzed into my office to let me know that not a single person in the venerable old firm's Los Angeles office had ever failed the California Bar exam and I certainly should not be the first. There is nothing quite like some unnecessary and in my opinion overtly nasty, additional pressure to really make one nervous. I found out several months later that this alleged "fact" wasn't actually true; it took one talented associate at the firm three attempts to pass. But the managing partner's revisionist historical rendition freaked me out sufficiently that I studied literally non-stop and with reckless abandon right up until ten minutes before the exam. Though knowing my Type-A self, I would probably have done that anyway, but perhaps without the sickening feeling in the pit of my stomach. It was a hellish, three-day-long stress-fest marathon in a hotel's massive grand ballroom near LAX. Fortunately, I passed on the first attempt, since I highly doubt I would have had the constitutional wherewithal to take it a second time. Thank goodness it wasn't a hypothetical theory I had to test in reality.

After a couple of days off to recuperate, I went back to work in earnest. The work was sophisticated, plentiful, and stimulating, and I had a lot of contact with Japanese business people, albeit not always in the way I had imagined. Often I would be asked to go into a conference room ostensibly to take notes on deal-point negotiations. The real reason was often to eavesdrop on what was being said by the Japanese business people to their counterparts, who had no clue that the blond westerner spoke anything other than English. It was kind of unfair, but business is business, and as they usually spoke both English and Japanese, more often than not, they had the unfair advantage. They would ultimately learn that I knew what was going on and, while often rather surprised, seemed fairly non plussed.

During those first six months, all was going well, though the first clear signs that there was something seriously wrong with this partner started to appear. Without a doubt, this man was a full-fledged screamer. By that I mean a blood-curdling, screeching, window-shaking screamer, verbally assaulting with reckless abandon whoever happened to piss him off at the moment or anyone who otherwise happened to appear in his airspace. Thus far I, thankfully, had never given him reason to take his wrath out on me, or simply was conveniently absent when his tirades transpired. But as my office was only two doors down from his, I had already heard enough to last an aural lifetime. One morning as I got up from my chair to drop off some lengthy document revisions on a complex transaction, I heard him screaming profusely at someone on the phone. This wasn't just loud screaming and cursing—which one can often hear at law firms, but a long-winded, highly offensive, and stinging personal attack. I had to pass by his office to get to the word-processing department at the other end of the hall. As I neared his office, out of his doorway flew the heavy, ten-inch Waterford crystal ashtray that normally sat on his desk. This airborne leaden torpedo missed my head by less than an inch. Stunned, I stopped short and looked at his long-time secretary who sat in the bay in front of his office, as if her facial expression might impart some rational explanation. She whispered something about medication and a bank department-head screwing up a Japan deal. I bolted for the word-processing department clenching my documents, like a bat flying out of a burning legal hell.

His behavior got more and more bizarre as the months went on, and his secretary told me on the sly that he was taking lithium, and if he didn't take a pill right on time at scheduled intervals, all hell would break loose. He would fly into these abusive and incredibly loud screaming rages, where his face would turn beet-red, and the veins on the sides of his neck would start to bulge; these fits would be directed at the offending party, usually a more junior lawyer, or a banker or escrow officer, or whoever else happened to be handy.

I recalled how he came into my office late one evening, around eight o'clock, and began screaming and cursing at the top of his lungs for what seemed like an eternity without stopping for a breath. I quickly realized, much to my relief, that I wasn't involved at all on the deal that had triggered his current hysterical tirade. I said nothing as I knew by then that interrupting him was pointless, or worse. (Besides, it gave me time to search my memory for the extension of the lawyer at the other end of the suite, who was about to get verbally gutted and guillotined.) On and on he went, ranting and raving, utterly out of control. When he finally did come up for air, although I was pretty shaken up, I told him as calmly as possible that I wasn't on the deal that was causing him such grief. He simply turned around and, without a single word of remorse, much less an apology, stomped out and headed toward the office of the poor guy who was. Immediately I grabbed the phone, called the other lawyer, and gave him the head's up. This was much like radio contact from one trench soldier to another during wartime, with a warning of incoming sniper fire, or in this case, a plethora of full-body grenades—except that our battlefield was a posh office suite with a view in a swanky part of town, and the enemy was our very own commanding officer, our "general." The other lawyer cornered me in the hallway the next day and thanked me, saying a bit sheepishly that he had quickly jumped into the stairwell near his office and walked down sixteen flights of stairs and grabbed a sandwich to avoid the certain incoming mortar-shell onslaught.

The problem with our general was that there were days when he was his normal, brilliant, charming self, smiling freely and making jokes, very often at his own expense. Or as a surprise, he'd have your favorite lunch delivered to your office, not just with a small dessert included, but with enough chocolate for a diabetes-inducing party. Or for no reason, he would generously bestow unexpected and expensive gifts. After a while I became somewhat immune to the Dr. Jekyll and Mr. Hyde routine. The fancy lunches and the gifts had no meaning to me and provided little salve, as I knew that lurking just around the corner was a venomous debt-collector who would eventually come calling with a vengeance in the form of the next uncalled-for outrage. Only here the usurious interest was twenty times any possible loan amount—and sometimes there hadn't even been a loan. As any experienced combat soldier worth his salt will tell you, even when the alleged enemy isn't firing live ammunition, you always have to be ready in the trenches and fully prepared for the sniper's onslaught. It is, to be sure, a very tough existence, and a truly miserable way to live.

One day, our general was positively swooning. I went to grab a coffee, and when I saw his secretary in the cafeteria, asked her tongue-in-cheek whether she had inadvertently upped his morning dose. She laughed and told me that he had recently ordered $30,000 worth of Italian furniture for his office, and it had just that morning arrived. She said the other partners weren't too happy about the extravagant expense and thought it excessive, but since his billings and collections the last few months were off the charts and way over projections, no one was making any direct noise.

The economy and business were booming, the practice got even busier, and our general hired a young lawyer from some small town in the Deep South. Those on our team were all a bit surprised at this selection given the nature of the team's practice. The newbie had only a few months of non-relevant legal experience, had never been west of the Mississippi until the job interview, and could not have found Asia on a world map had there been only two continents placed squarely upon it. But, we collectively thought, it was another warm body, and we were happy at potentially being able to pass off some of the burden of the never-ending workload. I later heard from a headhunter that the general always requested out-of-town candidates to interview. Perhaps this was because his unorthodox behavioral tendencies were better known in the local legal community.

For me, it was a Catch-22 situation. The work was interesting and demanding, I spent a lot of time with Japanese speakers and my language skills in the business context were rapidly sharpening. But the hours were very long, as is typical in large, national law firms, and the general's behavior so utterly unpredictable. I often felt like I was living in an insane asylum, albeit without the benefit of any resident PhDs in psychology, or at least a readily available straight jacket. Several months later, the general called me into his office wearing a big smile – clearly it was a good day – and he said he had "great news." A fairly large, California based law firm had made him an offer he couldn't refuse and they were extending offers to everyone on his team. He went on and on about all of the virtues of this other firm, only a few blocks away, but I had already stopped listening. My mind raced as I was simultaneously burning with fury at being faced with yet another impending merger so soon after my arrival, and at the same time relieved that he would be leaving. I thought perhaps I might be able to carve out a position with another partner at the firm and remain. Then the general dropped the decision-making bomb. Because the other firm was

California-based and not New York-based, his team members would all have to take a five-figure annual pay cut so that we would earn the same amount as the lock-step associates at the other firm. I told the general I would think about it for a few days, since, while I appreciated the offer, I wasn't thrilled about the prospect of leaving a large national law firm when I had arrived only a year before, or of reducing my salary.

No amount of imagination could possibly have prepared me for what transpired next, which can best be described as a fantastically flammable, highly hazardous and toxic explosion. He stood up from behind his desk and started screaming about what an ingrate I was, that this was a great opportunity for me professionally, but if I was too much of a stupid moron to see that, then he didn't want me to join him and would simply ask the Southerner to ride jump-seat.

I remember that I had to bite the inside of my lip almost to the point of bloodletting so that I didn't start laughing in this man's face. Here was this brilliant though completely crazy person asking me to join him at the other firm because I was smart and a valued and capable member of the team—indeed, the only one at the firm conversant in Japanese—yet at the same time he was calling me a stupid moron because I didn't want to make a snap professional decision with far-reaching consequences. The only moron in my mind at that moment would have been the Southerner if she agreed to go with the general. She did go probably because she was well-aware that no other partner at the firm would give her any work once the general left. In fact, as it turned out she was the only one who left with him.

I met with another partner in the same department, a soft-spoken and elegant man who detested the general and was only too happy to keep me busy. But he was a fairly junior partner, didn't have nearly the sophisticated work load or the volume and he wasn't too highly regarded at the firm. I stayed at this firm another year-and-a-half, just long enough so that another move would not murder my resume, then jumped at the chance to leave when an opportunity arose with another big law firm in Paris.

Three or four years later, I'd heard that the general's wife had their first child. He was in the delivery room at the time and, when the baby crowned, crashed to the floor and had a heart attack, which he survived. Two years after that, I heard that he and his wife had another baby. While his wife took a shower at the other end of the house, the general gave the three-month-old infant a bath in the kitchen sink. With the baby still in the water, he had a massive and fatal heart attack. Their housekeeper, who was in the next room, ran to the kitchen and saved the baby's life with just seconds to spare. A very sad ending to a very sad story.

As difficult as this experience was to endure—and it was very hard—it ultimately served me well. Not just because of the actual work experience, which was excellent, but also because it gave me a much clearer lens on what to avoid, if at all possible, in the future. Some lessons, though, are much harder to learn than others, and require continuing reinforcement in order to get through.

Years later I met an American attorney, raised working-class in New York and turned hugely successful businessman who had been resident for many years in Hong Kong. What a huge life this man had! He was well-traveled, well-read, cultured, spoke several languages, and had an amazing history of business success. He had a large cache of interesting, international mover-and-shaker friends, a chauffeured car, and an enormous, fully staffed home with a view of the entire Hong Kong harbor and skyline. He was warm, smart, funny, loved good food and wine, enjoyed exercise, could talk about interesting things long into the night, and loved to go to new places and try new things. Not a single blade of grass ever had the slightest chance of growing under this man's feet.

We got along great, it seemed like a really good match, our friends liked each other, and I was crazy about him and the life we were planning. So when he asked me to marry him a few months later, I happily said yes, and started making plans to move to Hong Kong. This was no small move, and there were a million details to attend to. He had a big staff in Hong Kong who could make that end of it easier, but many of the dreary details had to be done by me in the U.S. before I could leave.

Almost immediately after our lavish engagement party in Hong Kong, he started to exhibit many of the same traits that the general did. But this was harder for me to glean, since I wasn't spending every waking moment with him like I had with the general. For several months we were commuting back and forth—a week in Hong Kong, a week in the U.S. Or we would meet somewhere else for week or a long weekend. At first I thought I was losing my own mind, mainly because I just didn't want to acknowledge, much less believe, that this déjà vu experience was now invading my personal life. After several more months of unpredictable and often truly bizarre and obsessive behavior, which came to a head over the Christmas holidays in Thailand, I had had enough. As disgusting and morally demeaning as it is to be abused in a business setting—and I am not in any way, shape or form condoning that—it is altogether something else to be verbally abused and controlled in one's personal life. I knew I wouldn't survive another trip around that crazy-making mulberry bush. Even so, it was crushing for me emotionally.

I then found myself in the position of having to ask myself some really hard questions about myself and my life—about how I got to this point, along with what it was about me and my own character flaws that seemed to drive me at high-speed without stopping for gas right to the fast lane of this autobahn of manic, dangerous drivers. None of these questions came easily for me—neither the asking, nor the several lame attempts at answering, many of which failed miserably. It was a long and arduous process, and I stumbled around and stubbed my toes a few times in the difficult process. Finally, I came to the realization that in both my professional life and my personal one, I had made the very same mistakes in terms of the kind of company I was attracted to and thus kept in my inner circle. This had certainly hindered me professionally, and very nearly crippled me personally. I was the perpetual wing woman riding *behind* the jump seat. I was never a flight engineer or a co-captain, much less a full-fledged pilot in the 747 of my own life. Whatever I did, either at work or at home, was designed to make someone else look better, shine brighter, be happier or be more successful, much to my own detriment. And simply put, it was ruining me and killing even the possibility of any chance for real happiness in either arena. It was time for a real and drastic change. It was high time, now or never really, to take a deep breath, and attempt to find myself in the company of those who could honestly share some of the oxygen in my life. Not only so I could draw breath, but also so that I could exhale—however it looked—and at the same time truly be a bit more than the witty, ghost-writing, window dressing I had somehow become. I wanted no longer to gasp for a mere half-breath of thin air.

Once I fully understood what it was that I really needed, the internal seismic shift took on, it seemed, a life all its own. At a speed I can still hardly grasp, things suddenly fell into place, piece by piece, and both personal and professional aspects of my life turned a remarkable corner. When I decided to leave the law firm I was with at the time, several high-quality clients unexpectedly asked me if I would take them on as I had decided to work for myself. About a year later, I met the man who would truly share life with me and, in rather short order, I married him. This period often left me breathless, but for the first time in my life, the sensation of breathlessness was akin to that experienced by someone one who was happily finishing a marathon for which she'd trained hard, not the gasping wheezes of a runner who was choking to death at the five-mile marker.

Though far easier said than done, we need regularly to take a good look at the component parts which make up the totality of our lives. We must make sure that we do not surround ourselves with asphyxiating, demoralizing, pain-dispensing people.

This kind of soul searching is critical, regardless of how attractively seductive those oxygen stealers may seem at first blush. Instead, we must ask and then answer the difficult questions so that we can find a way to surround ourselves with life-enhancing, oxygen-producing, pain-relieving people. Those people who are not only able to allow air to freely circulate in your world and permit the shared relief of exhalation, but those who actually revel in the shared blossom of joy which results, and the fine scent that it produces.

17

Recent technological advances have been enormous and often wonderful aids in our busy and complicated lives. One must, though, regularly disconnect from this double-edged sword of benefit and burden.

I recall with fondness my mother recounting stories of the old man on the rickety truck yelling, *"Kerach, Kerach*!!!" (Ice, Ice!!!) as he drove slowly through the neighborhood in Tel-Aviv where she grew up. The *kerach* was used for the old ice boxes before modern refrigeration was a reality. Similar stories came from my father's mother and her recollections of keeping house without a washing machine and the now antiquated methods of ironing clothes in Vienna where she grew up and lived until the onset of WWII. Fast-forward to that woman's now eighty-seven-year-old daughter, keeping in touch with me and others on her shiny, one-year-old iPad. And I sit at this very moment on Gili Trawangan, a tiny speck of an island in the middle of the Indian Ocean, far away from home or the noise, crowds and carbon-monoxide-filled air of Jakarta and Denpasar. There are only two methods of transportation on Gili Trawangan. One is ancient—horse-drawn carriages, used mainly for luggage transport from the boat launch where one arrives; the other is very old—one-speed bicycles, mainly without brakes. And I am typing away on a three-pound netbook and keeping in touch with loved ones afar via Skype. That is, when the wifi is working. My, my, how times have changed.

The changes, nearly all positive in my profession as a lawyer, have been monumental—from black, manual typewriters with correction tape, to IBM Correcting Selectrics and Dictaphones, to computers. Computers, of course, have changed the nature of litigation practice of my colleagues in those specialties, permitting ease of drafting, redrafting and editing of one's arguments and briefs. The flipside is repetitive, lengthy briefs where some attorneys are under the misconception that length, breadth and weight have something to do with clarity, brevity and articulate, persuasive writing. This is now so prevalent that courts in all U.S. jurisdictions have had to set up specific limits on the number of pages permitted for submission of documents to the courts. Also now readily available online are legal forms for both lawyers and lay people, as well as e-filing for certain court documents.

Then there is e-mail. What e-mail has done for business negotiations and transactions is nothing short of mind-boggling. On the positive side, it of course allows us to stay connected in both the local and global arenas, doing deals suitable to our own time zones (or at three a.m. local time if the deal simply must get done), so that when your foreign counterpart wakes up and signs on, he or she can dive right in and get to work without a moment—dollar, pound, rupiah or yen—to lose.

Here's an odd example of the human touch/feel disconnect. For over three years, I had communicated with a senior escrow officer of a large national company almost daily by e-mail on several deals, in totality to the tune of hundreds of millions of dollars. The e-mails, often with lengthy attachments, were full of deal points, and minute calculations and were quite detailed. When things got particularly complicated or I started to get cross-eyed, one of us, usually me, would finally pick up the phone to get clarity or attempt to wrap things up more speedily. During those three years, in order to break the often mind-numbing monotony of certain aspects of the transactions we worked on together, we would throw in a few morsels about our personal lives: upcoming vacations, discussions about our kids, husbands and the like. It's remarkable how open one can be when it's a telephone and not a live person sitting across from you. If anyone had asked me or her, we would have attested to a fairly close friendship. This was so despite the fact that we had never, ever actually met face-to-face, even though her office was a mere ten miles away from mine. However, in Los Angeles, ten miles was more like a hundred in the parking lot that the city's freeways and surface street arteries most often resembled. After three years and countless time-consuming transactions, unbeknownst to us, we were both invited to the same Christmas party at a Westside hotel. When a mutual colleague introduced us during the cocktail hour, we hugged each other like long-lost college roommates. The colleague who had "introduced" us, and who had assumed we didn't know each other, looked at us like we had both beamed down directly from some alien planet. It was both hilarious and, simultaneously, a bit sad. We vowed then and there to meet routinely and keep in real touch. One should never underestimate the value of being face-to-face, or indeed a good hug.

On the personal side, the electronic age permits us to stay connected with spouses away on business, kids off at summer camp, away traveling or off at college. It allows us to check from the other side of the globe that the dog sitter has given the right amount of phenobarbital to the epileptic pooch and make sure that the gardener remembered to lock the back gate. Match.com, the popular on-line dating site, now reports on its ever-present commercials that one of every five relationships begins from its readily available 24/7 services. And I'm not even talking about the Blackberry-addicted—and admittedly I was once one of those "Crackberry" addicts. I have since recovered very nicely thank you very much, even though I still possess one.

But what does this all really mean in the big picture? To be sure, many things are now simpler. You can order groceries from the comfort of your office chair, send your secretary flowers for her birthday at the very last minute, and buy plane tickets to anywhere—including, as Sir Richard Branson will no doubt soon see to it, to the moon—as well as anything else that one might want or need. However, it also means that we are never really permitted to disconnect psychically, to vacate or to clear our minds, even temporarily, from all that that clutters them. The word *vacation* has, at its root, the concept of vacating— obviously to empty out, to clear, to see things anew. All of the technology is really wonderful. And as easy as it has made certain things to accomplish on a traffic-congested and often frenetically paced planet, it will never, in my opinion, make up for opening up a real handwritten letter from your mail carrier, hearing a loved one's voice on a real telephone, seeing someone laugh heartily, or, better yet, being on the receiving end of a real, live kiss. Heart-shaped emoticons notwithstanding.

While walking through a night market in Hong Kong with our teenaged daughter recently, which had at its overflowing stalls virtually everything from trademark-infringing handbags to ancient appliances, we happened upon an old black rotary dial telephone. The precise kind I grew up with, long before wall mounts and fashionably colored princess phones came into vogue. My daughter stopped, stared and looked utterly perplexed in a way that only a teenager can. "How did that thing work?" she shrieked. As I showed her how the dial worked, she tried it a couple of times, but struggled with the finger holes of the rotary dial. Mind you, this is a kid who can, virtually within minutes of opening up a box of digital anything, and without even considering opening the enclosed manual, make a gadget speedily beam to life without blinking an eye.

The benefits of modern technology have been enormous, and, for the most part, wonderful. I, of course, would never want to return to life without a washing machine. That said, with the benefits of modern technology comes a corresponding burden: the inability to disconnect from constant availability, distraction and interruption. So unplug, disconnect, go off-line, get up, or, as Ma Bell used to advertise constantly in the days when real telephones ruled the rotary-dial roost, "reach out and touch someone." Or better yet, give someone a kiss. Though preferably, perhaps, someone you know.

18

Opposites often attract in unimaginable ways.
Enjoy the ride.

One would think that having an important relationship or marrying someone with more similarities to than differences from you would make it easier to get along and survive the many bumps that occur on the road of life. Often that is the case, but certainly not always. Sometimes love can bloom, survive and thrive even among those with vastly different upbringings and experiences and can make as wonderful a match as peanut butter and jelly.

My husband and I could not possibly be more different. While we are both lawyers and both have Type-A personalities, that pretty much is where our similarities end. When we first started dating, we used to joke that we were so different that our collective friends must have thought we were utterly insane to date though we both realized very early on in our courtship that together we had something unique. This was made crystal clear to us one evening at a restaurant in Mexico when, after ordering our food, we had spent nearly thirty minutes intensely discussing the relative virtues of using semi-colons in legal writing. Admittedly, most normal people would have preferred a quick death by a Russian firing squad rather than be party to *that* conversation. The two of us, however, were on the punctuation/grammar induced equivalent of an amorous cloud nine.

As to the more obvious differences, he's tall, I'm short. He was raised Catholic, I was raised Jewish. He grew up in New York and came from a traditional Irish Catholic family of five kids, with a dad who went to work every day and a stay-at-home mom who ruled the roost. I was basically an only child with a single working parent and grew up as far west as you could get and still be in the U.S. My husband always had lots of people around his house when he was growing up, and then also in college and at law school. Mine was a much more solitary experience, and, as I got older and went off to college and then law school, I found that I preferred living alone or with one roommate, rather than in a group house.

However, despite the glaringly obvious differences—and they were and remain many—we ultimately found that, deep down, many comforting similarities surfaced in the face of those significant differences. And where the differences were so different as to be seemingly insurmountable, we often found that each of us had a lesson to learn as adults that we could not possibly have learned as children or teenagers. As a result, we and the family we created benefited in unimaginable ways.

Take the Catholic/Jewish divide, for example. At first blush, one would think that there are zero similarities. However, as one digs just below the surface, the basic tenets of most Christian denominations are, of course, very similar to those of Judaism. And between all of the collective Jewish and Catholic guilt in our respective religions, we have so much to spare that we've often considered selling it at a bulk discount to Buddhists or Taoists who may be sorely lacking in that regard. But seriously, it does help, of course, that neither one of us is religious. I can't even remember the last time I stepped into a synagogue for the purposes of prayer, and he has gone to a church service exactly once in the years I've known him.

Truth be told, the almighty, non-religious, manic marketing Christmas tree is still extremely important to him. So every year, right after Thanksgiving, we go out and do the unthinkably un-green thing and buy a real, live Christmas tree. My annual pleas to purchase an artificial tree of any size fall on consistently deaf ears. Never mind that one of our dogs routinely uses the tree as her very personal, very tall green urinal, and the other dog practically choked to death one year after attempting to digest a few choice glass ornaments. For him the tree signifies all that is good about childhood, about hope and about humanity. For me, the tree signifies my personal contribution to global warming—sigh—at least two new vacuum cleaner bags—ugh—and a potentially urgent call to one of those seriously handsome calendar centerfolds at the local fire station. Hmmm, well I suppose *that* wouldn't be so terrible. But perhaps most importantly, the Christmas tree signifies deep and abiding love. I can thus go through the messy motions which have virtually no meaning to me with gusto and enthusiasm, because I know just how important it is to him.

I recall the first time we had a Christmas tree in our home. It was a large seven-foot affair which we carefully maneuvered into the family room off of our kitchen. We then decorated every inch of it with reckless abandon. I will never forget walking down the stairs the next morning at the crack of dawn and stopping abruptly in my tracks and thinking incredulously, "Oy vey, I'm Jewish! Who on God's green earth put a Christmas tree in my house and then had the chutzpah to decorate the blasted thing while I was sleeping???!!!" Oh the things you do for love.

Since I grew up as an only child with a single parent, I pretty much always knew where everything was in my childhood home. It was exactly where my mom or I had last put it. And because there were only two of us, keys, purses and the like rarely got lost or misplaced. Although my mother did have a strange habit of searching frantically through the house for her glasses, only to finally find them squarely perched on the top of her head. Also, since for many years it was just the two of us, and we were such different sizes, neither had to worry about our clothes or shoes mysteriously ending up in another one's closet. And unless there were colleagues of my mom's around, it was also fairly quiet. We didn't watch much television, but read quite a bit and there usually was some light classical music on in the background. Or my mom would play the piano, which she could do by ear. Thus I had perhaps more physical order as a child and teenager than my husband ever could have had in his busy house growing up. That sense of order became my norm and my comfort zone.

With four siblings, my husband, on the other hand, had a vastly different upbringing. Though my mother-in-law no doubt ran a supremely tight, Catholic-inspired ship, five children and two adults in one house with two bathrooms are a whole lot of warm bodies with which to contend. So the ability to be flexible and to adapt became a survival skill of the "sibling masses." As a result, my husband is far more tolerant than I could ever be in terms of the noise level or magnitude of distraction that he can live with. Or, for that matter, whether he wears his socks or a pair belonging to one of the teenagers. Often he doesn't even notice decibel levels that would in short order send me to an audiologist with an electric-shock-therapy chaser. I can come home to find every single light on in the house, with him working in the den on some voluminous pleadings, with CNN on loudly in the background. As that is happening, one teenager is playing online computer games with an Estonian friend and the volume screeching on full tilt, while another one is upstairs watching some hormone-induced teenage rom com, and a college kid home on break is simultaneously watching the Blitz at deafening levels on the history channel and loudly Skyping God-knows-who, only God knows where. The dogs, of course are chasing each other back and forth across the house over an ancient and deformed scary-looking stuffed animal, and when one finally triumphs, they engage in a growling tug-of-war match that ends only when a stuffed limb has been duly amputated and the limb's contents have been spewed into their water dish. And into this total cacophony of chaos I walk and am greeted with my husband's big smile and a deep kiss as if I had just arrived and am being warmly welcomed into the Garden of Eden.

I am certain my husband can recount the numerous ways he has had to adapt (and adapt he most generously has), to my "neatnik" tendencies, sense of order and preference for controlled decibel levels, but thankfully he is not the one penning a book about the many lessons he has learned. In all seriousness, though, we have come together from the most disparate backgrounds and experiences and learned not only to appreciate our differences and revel in the similarities out of a deep and profound love, friendship and respect for one another, but also to raise a small army of pretty cool kids, who could not be more different from each other. So while partnering with those of similar background and experience is certainly one way to ride though life, and is often far easier, sometimes the lessons to be learned by partnering with one who is more different from than similar to you can provide some additional avenues for growth, comfort and respect, as does living with the almighty and greatest equalizer of all times, love. Victor Hugo knew precisely what he was talking about when he wrote, "The supreme happiness of life is the conviction that we are loved." Similar or different, the same or opposite, *mon cher Victor,* this is a conviction I will gladly take to heart every single day of my life.

19

Sometimes not getting what you think you desperately want is precisely what you need.

A few months before my husband and I got married, we spent a lazy, sunny afternoon driving around the area where we were going to live after the wedding. Naturally, because we weren't really looking to buy, we found the perfect house for sale. Everything in it was exactly where it was supposed to be and was picture-perfect. The hardwood floors were gleaming, the granite kitchen was beautiful and opened up to a lovely family room with a view of the postage-stamp-sized, but lushly landscaped backyard. We even liked the seller's furnishings and artwork.

Although we weren't really house hunting that day, or even really ready to buy at that moment, we both fell in love with that house. And as is known to happen to even the most rational and logical of people, our collective brains went into real estate overdrive. My house was already in escrow and would soon close, but my fiancé's house didn't yet have a buyer. The seller's market was fairly soft at the time, and there was no guarantee his house would sell, much less close escrow by the time the owners of the house we wanted needed to move back east.

As my fiancé's workload at the office was all-consuming, and my schedule was more within my control, selling his house was not only left to me, but became my temporary holy mission in life. Over the next six weeks, I did everything imaginable to get his house into escrow. The price was lowered twice, I emptied closets with reckless abandon and had two garage sales to get rid of the stuff—and, my goodness, was there a ton of stuff.

What didn't sell at the garage sales – and nearly everything, I'm glad to say, did—was hauled out and tossed into one of the two enormous dumpsters in the driveway that I had rented. I then picked out new paints, new light fixtures and new hardware for the entire house and bought new toilets and mirrors for all of the bathrooms, had the Jacuzzi tub re-glazed, ordered new shower doors and shower heads, selected new carpet for the bedrooms and oversaw all of the laborers' work and installations. There were several pieces of excess furniture which I had moved into the garage, and I staged what remained in the house. I then bought fifteen-dozen flats of colorful flowers and several trees for the gardener and his crew to plant. The pool man cleaned and scrubbed the pool and deck until it was gleaming. The manager at the nearby Home Depot – which I had alternately renamed Home Desperation or Home Despot, depending on my mood – commented to me one afternoon that he saw me there so often, he was considering giving me my own parking space. I certainly wish he had, though sadly he never did. I did everything under the sun short of offering a new car and a tropical vacation to the broker who would produce a ready, willing and able buyer. Frankly though, had I thought of that then, I probably would have done that too. Despite all of my time-consuming and seemingly ultra-heroic efforts, the frustrating reality was that his house was simply not going to sell in that market at any price, other than as a charitable contribution, which we had already made to our maximum that year. It drove us practically insane, as we were so anxious to move on with our lives, and that house felt like an old and heavy ball-and-chain around our betrothed necks.

We then engaged in some creative methods of mental financing and figured we could still buy the new house even if his house didn't sell. We could instead lease his house out long-term while we waited for the market to rebound. So we marched on with renewed fervor down that potentially slippery slope.

The first prospective tenants were a man, his fiancé and her two children. Their application looked good, they were financially solvent and their credit reports came back in order. I drafted the lease, and the night before they were to sign it, the man's fiancé got wind that his ex-wife had just leased a house around the corner. They sheepishly backed out and our roller-coaster ride continued. We stayed in touch with the seller's broker on the house we wanted, keeping her apprised of our continuing efforts.

The second prospective tenants were two late middle-aged spinster sisters and their elderly mother, referred by someone from a nearby church. My fiancé spoke at length to one of the sisters, a sweet lady who was certain the house would be "just perfect" for them. The real estate agent showed them the house two days later, they all loved it and they took the application home to complete. We received the application piecemeal over the course of the next week; perhaps they thought this way we might not notice that they wouldn't be able to afford the utilities, much less the rent. They had virtually no savings, only one sister had a part-time job with a very modest income, and they had a collective credit score teetering on bankruptcy.

A week later my fiancé's agent called and said he would be showing the house the next morning to another prospective tenant. This one was "pre-screened and top notch," he said. That same afternoon the broker on the house we wanted to buy also called. She told me that the house we loved and desperately wanted to buy had just entered escrow. We were just crestfallen.

As it turned out, and just like the nursery rhyme of Goldilocks and the three bears, the third prospective tenants were just right. They loved the house, were gainfully employed, and had great credit. They paid the rent with the reliability of Big Ben, and were all-around every landlord's dream tenants.

Since the house we had so badly wanted to buy had sold, and our wedding was just a few weeks away, we gave up on the idea of buying another house at that time. There was too much going on, and there was just no time to spare. But soon neither of us would have a place to live. As I was reminding my fiancé of this minor detail late one night and starting to hyperventilate with a myriad of details swimming in my head, as blind luck would have it, he took to the papers, made a few calls, and immediately found what sounded like the perfect house for us to lease, close to the beach. It sounded too perfect—and part of me couldn't believe that it had taken him literally ten minutes of searching—but I raced down the next day anyway, and sure enough, it was perfect in every respect. I called him from the kitchen of that house and he, trusting my real estate judgment, told me to lease it, though he hadn't seen it. I signed the papers right then and there and we moved in ten days later, two months before the wedding.

While living in that great rental, we had walked nearly every inch of the neighborhood and the surrounding ones. If I had a dollar for every time one of us said how lucky we were that his house hadn't sold that summer, we would have had enough money for round-trip tickets for us to renew our marital vows at Elvis' Chapel of Love in Las Vegas, with enough left over to feed a nearby one-armed bandit. As it turned out, we ended up just detesting the street the original house was on, finally noticing that it was too close to the freeway, one neighbor had perpetual exterior Christmas lights hung, and another had a consistent overflow of garbage often threatening to take over their driveway.

While we were nearly driven to drink that summer when we couldn't sell his house to save our souls, now we wanted to drink in celebration and good fortune that it hadn't. What a difference a few months makes. And we really enjoyed living in that rental and became very friendly with the owner, the former mayor of the town who, with a phone call, could get you any information you needed about the town or any business or person in it. It also allowed us, of course, the time and ability to make a much better, more-thoughtful and less-rushed decision on such an enormous and important purchase. So just when you think you will lose your mind because you don't get what you think you so desperately want, and it is far easier said than done to stay objective when you're in the thick of things, wait a few months. It may just turn out that what you get is exactly what you really need.

20

Just like an appendix, everyone has a built-in, self-preserving, inner alarm system. Make sure the batteries are charged so that you can hear it when it goes off.

If you, or anyone you know, has ever had an acute attack of appendicitis, the warning signs are normally pretty clear. They include an onset of fever, nausea, vomiting and an aching pain in the lower right side of the abdomen that becomes sharper over several hours. This is usually followed by a quick trip to a physician and then a swift introduction to a surgeon and anesthesiologist, then admission to a hospital for an even swifter appendectomy. No one wants the inflamed appendix to burst, as the potentially resulting peritonitis and shock can be fatal.

We have generally become accustomed to listening to the warning bells our bodies often use to signal us when something is physically wrong, and hopefully we take the appropriate action. We are often far less able, however, to tune into the other internal warning bells that we all have within us concerning things we should or shouldn't do in our lives.

Those other internal warning bells have been given a host of names: gut feeling, inner voice or intuition, just to name a few. But whatever you want to call it, one thing is clear: you should take heed of its signs and warnings in the same way that you would a raging case of appendicitis. Your judgment has been tuned and well-honed over the years. Not listening to it—or worse, ignoring it altogether—can cause an incredible amount of grief after the fact, or worse.

Listening to your intuition is not easy to do. We are a society of veritable second-guessers, always seeking out the opinions of others and analyzing things and events from a hundred possible different angles. This often permits the suppression of our own internal warning-bell system, to our ultimate detriment. And it seems this has actually become more acute with the availability of internet chat rooms and blogging, as the pool of available opinions has increased a million fold and is there for our perusal literally around the clock.

The fact is that your personal intuition is the wisest and very best sage you will ever have the pleasure of knowing. This is not always the logical right-side of the brain, the loud voice you are, more often than not, accustomed to hearing, and whose directions you usually follow. It is the *other* voice—the one that just sort of quietly nags at you when you are busy paying attention and listening to the logical, loud, right-side-of-the-brain voice. Intuition is like a muscle; the more you use it, the more it is strengthened and developed. The degree to which you dial into it is entirely up to you. The most important thing is that you actually *trust* your intuition. I am not talking about blindly trusting snap judgments, but trusting the very first authentic feelings you have about a person, choice or event. Those often-quiet, authentic feelings if you are able to dial into them, are usually the right ones for you.

Often, not following our instincts can have catastrophic outcomes, as history has shown us. Calpurnia Pisonis was a Roman woman and the third and final wife of Julius Caesar. They married in late 59 B.C. when Calpurnia was just sixteen years old. In 44 B.C., according to some ancient sources, Calpurnia had a premonition of Caesar's assassination, and she tried in vain to warn him. She also encouraged Decimus Junius Brutus Albinus, Caesar's distant cousin, to send word to the Senate that Caesar was sick that day. However, sadly for Caesar, he refused to lie that he was ill and went ahead. Thus the Ides of March came and went, and with it, the life of Julius Caesar. If only he had listened to Calpurnia! Many, many moons later and across the great pond, Ulysses S. Grant was invited in 1865 to go to the Ford Theater in Washington, D.C. with Abraham Lincoln to see the play *Our American Cousin.* For reasons unknown to Ulysses' wife Julia, she was fiercely adamant that Ulysses not attend the show, writing after the fact, "I do not know what possessed me to take such a freak." Fortunately for Ulysses' long-term health outlook, he took Julia's odd premonition quite seriously and did not attend the play. Not only was Ulysses spared from having to bear witness to Lincoln's assassination, but it was later determined that he too had been a potential target. Thus, in hindsight, Julia may have saved her husband's life, not to mention unwittingly altered American history.

While I can't say that I have knowingly kept anyone from being assassinated, certainly in my own life, my intuition has served me well. That was certainly the case when my internal warning bell went off I was traveling on a dark patch of foreign mountain road, as I did that scary night in the Philippines when I attached myself to the gracious Roman Catholic nun. It has also occurred while working when, I felt an internal, inexplicable insistence that more research needed to be done for a client simply because something was nagging at me, and that bit of extra research ended up saving the day. Where my own inner voice has come in the loudest and clearest over the years, however, has been in relation to, well, relationships.

There was a period in my life when it often seemed that I simply refused to listen to my intuition, most notably with the Surgeon Who Wasn't and with disastrous results. During that long period, it was almost as if I could see the train crashing head-on into the station, and yet I was powerless to get out of the sleeping car. That, of course, was not true; I was certainly physically and financially more than able to get out of the car. But at that time I chose instead to listen to the self-imposed and loud rationalization that surfaced mostly, I believe, because I so desperately wanted things to be and turn out a certain way. So to suppress the nagging voice within, which in fairness did try to make itself heard, I would recite to myself a continuing litany of loud fictions—"He will get help, he will get a job, he will participate in his own life," etc. This was the case even when all of the evidence was fully contradictory to my best hopes and aspirations. There did come a day, thankfully, though it was many years later, when I finally did take heed of the inner voice—though when that day finally came, that usually quiet inner voice ultimately became more like a three-alarm fire bell. It was almost as if my inner voice's normally low-grade hum was sick and tired of neglect and finally screamed, "ENOUGH ALREADY!!!" Better I paid attention later than never, of course, but I certainly could have saved myself a mountain of grief had I simply paid more attention earlier to my wise inner voice.

That lengthy and painful experience led me to listen much more carefully to my inner voice. And thereafter, I found it easier to hear it without having to wait until the proverbial scream occurred or someone (usually me) was figuratively bleeding. Or worse.

On the positive side, as I became more cognizant and trusting of my inner voice, I found that it was actually a constant companion on my journey through life. As time went on, I also learned that my inner voice was completely trustworthy, inherently reliable and brutally honest, just like a really good friend who had my best interests at heart. But it wasn't all smooth sailing. There was a lot of fun in my life, though it was sprinkled with a few more relationships in which I ignored my inner voice with ghastly results. But with these at least, when the inner voice kicked in, I paid attention. So while I was still making some mistakes in terms of the choices I was making, it didn't take me nearly as long to wake up and smell the proverbial coffee.

A couple of years after I started really trying to pay attention to the voice within, I was supposed to meet someone for a quick, thirty-minute drink after work. Nearly four hours, two glasses of wine and a several-course dinner later, my inner voice was so busy and so happy, it was nearly as loud as the logical, right-side-of-the brain voice. Happily, my companion asked me for a second date before the first one was over. As I was driving home that night, my inner voice was wildly dancing a jig to what seemed like very loud music. And my inner voice's dance partner was my logical right-side brain! I simply knew intuitively then that I was about to embark on an amazing journey with this man who was and remains completely perfect *for me*. And that is exactly what has transpired. Only now that man is my husband.

Just like the physical signs our bodies give us when physiological trouble is lurking around the corner, we need to pay at least the same amount of attention when our internal psychological warning bells go off. Learning to dial-in and take heed may save you a ton of heartache, or at least loads of trouble. Keeping those batteries charged and your internal engine tuned to hear its quiet hum may also bring you to a place where you can clearly see exactly what you need when the grace of good fortune crosses your path.

21

Your childhood experiences will likely determine the way you earn, save and spend money. Embrace your inner employee, banker and accountant.

A few months following my parents' divorce, my mother had to run an errand after work and asked me to accompany her. Dressed in her work suit, off we went to the local J.C. Penney's. She picked out a few pairs of hose for work and we went to the cashier. Although my mother had cash on hand, she informed the cashier that she wanted to open up a credit card account. She was handed an application, which she completed while standing at the counter. What then transpired had such an impact on me that it remains as clear as a bell in my mind, now forty-one years later. The cashier then called the manager on the phone, who promptly arrived at the cashier's counter. The manager then loudly informed my mother, well within the earshot of the other early-evening customers, that as a matter of company policy, J.C. Penney's did not give credit to divorced women, even if they were gainfully employed and even if they earned a living wage. If I live to be a 110, I will never, ever forget the look of shock, disbelief and humiliation that evening on my mother's face.

Yes, it was the autumn of 1969. Yes, divorced, professional women were not the norm. Yes, that manager was a jerk. And yes, that may in fact have been the "company policy" of J.C. Penney's at the time. But still, even after all the intervening years, that experience still has an impact on me, despite my understanding of those times. It long-ago affected my perceptions of creditworthiness, which I hold as near and dear to me as a delicious and rich hot fudge sundae. It affects how I treat my credit card bills—which I have paid off in full each month, even during my very leanest years, lest, heaven forbid, I pay even a nickel's service charge or cause a dime's interest to accrue. It affects how I balance my checkbook—as soon as I get the monthly bank statement—even if I am flush to the point of passing out, for fear, no matter how irrational, that I might bounce a check. Likewise, I pay my taxes on time and have never had to request a filing extension. I am not attempting to extol some kind of monetary virtue. *Au contraire*. It is just that I could never in a million years subject myself to even the merest possibility that I would have five seconds of those feelings that my mother endured that autumn evening at J.C. Penney's. Never.

The upside, of course, is that credit card companies continuously stuff my mailbox with never-ending offers of credit cards readily providing truly obscene credit limits—as if I would EVER charge that much money on a credit card! With the amount of paper I have to shred and then toss, those credit card companies are probably responsible for a good percentage of the depletion of the Amazon's rain forests. In the same vein, banks and mortgage companies have stumbled over each other with very favorable rates each time I have applied for a loan, whether for a car, a home, or something else. And of course I have never, not once, bounced a check. No surprise there, given the number of paper cuts I've gotten over the years, so rapidly did I open my bank statements to balance my checkbook.

That my mother went off to work every single morning of my childhood dressed and coiffed, sometimes racing around the house so as not to be even a minute late for a meeting or other work-related obligation, likewise affected me deeply. It was not simply financial independence and the ability to drive the bus of one's own destiny that thus propelled her, but what it meant to her deep inside, and by osmosis, to me, to be gainfully employed. It was her opinion that being employed, regardless of in what capacity, was the highest human calling. It was the same from her perspective if that calling was as a school janitor or as a research scientist. It just didn't matter. What did matter was that you did that job, whatever it was, to the very best of your ability, and that you appreciated the opportunities it presented—whether that opportunity was to feed and clothe your family or to find a cure for cancer. As a result, every time I worked for someone else, I recalled those concepts, perhaps especially so when the work was particularly monotonous or difficult.

I remembered that lesson clearly when just a few days into a new job as a mid-level attorney, a senior partner handed me a box containing several thick files of a corporation's financial data and asked me to locate the needle in the proverbial haystack in search of some obscure expenditures and reimbursements that a lender was seeking on the eve of a huge portfolio refinancing. Never mind that I had no accounting background and knew precious little about the company in question or its relevant history. When I expressed my perceived limitations to the partner, he simply said, "If everybody could do this kind of work, then this firm wouldn't be paying you what you are earning." He, of course, was right. It took me half the night, new batteries for my calculator, and a veritable gallon of caffeine to slog through the massive files. But ultimately I found the needed data and the deal closed on time. I did end up, however, with a new-found respect for accounting, though with less-than-zero desire ever to revisit that eye-crossing, mind-numbing experience. The next day I threw out my calculator, which finally died after the second time I spilled coffee on it. I also hired a new accountant.

The same can be said for how, and to what extent, one saves money. Our childhood experiences, whether one grows up with a silver spoon and funds to spare, or is raised with just enough to survive, have an everlasting impact on our monetary psyche. It affects how and to what extent one saves or spends, and its inherent financial corollary, one's levels of risk tolerance. To prove my financial neurosis, while just twenty-five years old

139

and still in law school, I'm pretty sure I shocked into an early retirement the assistant manager at the bank where I had my anemic checking account one afternoon when I requested that she deduct twenty-five dollars a month and deposit it into an IRA. The childhood experiences one has naturally also affect of course, what one teaches about money to one's children. As the child of a single, hard-working parent, I am by nature a saver, always a bit worried about the rainy day, which of course may come no matter how much one saves or doesn't save. I am also on the lower end of the spectrum of risk tolerance. Or, as is the case with most lawyers I know, basically risk averse. I may never get rich, but I will never be poor either. And that's just fine with me.

The bottom line is that coming to grips with these early experiences and understanding their genesis allows one to navigate the sometimes-stormy waters that can rise when one joins forces with another. And that is the case whether the joining of forces involves a work partnership with a colleague, or a familial partnership with one's spouse.

Though my husband was raised in a traditional family with more security than I had growing up, there were five children and just one modest salary. Thus, my mother-in-law became an expert *extraordinaire* in making dollars and meals stretch, and then stretch some more. All five of the children, when they became teenagers, had summer and after-school jobs. And all five children went off to college (to the cost of which they contributed through part-time jobs), became responsible adults, and are gainfully and successfully employed in their respective professions. That said, my husband's childhood memories of not having the "extras" more readily available to him while in high school, college and law school, still sometimes leave him today with a feeling of having "an old man on his back." We often joke about his "old man" being in cahoots, cavorting, and slumming with my "old woman pushing along a shopping cart full of all her earthly belongings in a parking lot."

In all likelihood for us as a couple, the reality of the "old man" and the "old woman," other than the marching on of Father Time, will never come to pass. Nevertheless, the fears that the "old man" and the "old woman" possess are very real, borne of our earliest childhood experiences. Understanding these experiences has allowed us to come to terms with them and to make financial decisions together that make sense for us and are within our mutual comfort zones. Make no mistake— we do not always agree on all of these issues, but for the most part, we do. And when we disagree on a particular item or strategy, we are better able to weather it because we understand the disagreement's similar genesis and can empathize with the underlying issue at hand.

So to all of this I say, boldly embrace your inner employee, banker and accountant. Sometimes even a big, sloppy kiss is in order. Your views on earning, saving and spending came from a plethora of childhood experiences that left its mark on your financial and fiscal heart and soul many moons ago. In other words, you have arrived at where you are today from, financially speaking, precisely whence you came. Understanding that winding, sometimes-convoluted financial journey you took will lead you not only to have compassion for the "old man on the back" and the "old woman with the shopping cart," but will probably also give you some great fodder for truly absurd jokes to share along the financial highway and byway of life.

22

**Success isn't the key to happiness; happiness is.
If you love what you're doing, you will be successful.**

In a murder mystery I once read, one of the plot's crime victims, a literary editor, said, not long before getting killed off, "I don't think anyone sets out in the world to be an editor. It's something that happens to you, like food poisoning or getting hit by a truck."

Admittedly, I know precious little about the literary publishing world, but I'm fairly certain that entering or staying in that profession, or any other one, for that matter, doesn't happen by pure chance. If it did then I might still be asking the age-old, golden-arch question of whether you want fries with that Big Mac and Coca-Cola.

Success, of course, can be defined in as many ways as there are apple varieties. One person's vision of success could be another person's clear-as-a-summer's day view of Purgatory. Success, by definition, just like beauty, is in the eyes of the beholder.

After working hard as an undergraduate, I was able to snag a full scholarship to attend a good law school on the east coast. In an era of dwindling graduate school funding, this was, at the time, nothing short of major miracle. I had toyed the year before with going to medical school, but after spending those two months in and out of the hospital with my terminally ill mother, I decided that despite the good I could potentially do, at least in theory, in the field of public health, I was not willing to spend much of my life in a hospital. And so off I went to law school, feeling pretty convinced I was on the right path, and also feeling very lucky to have the opportunity.

I wasn't there very long when I started to think I had made a monumental mistake. My first semester was less than stellar. I was slogging through my first real winter, I was homesick for the islands, and I was still grieving for the loss of my mother. I made an appointment to speak with one of the few women professors then at the law school—an older, chain-smoking, criminal law professor in whose class I did better than in some of the others I was taking. I can't now remember the exact words she said, and hers was certainly not an altogether-Victorian approach of "only paths of thorns lead to glory," but it had to do with opportunities lost and found, and not being a quitter if success didn't come in the first fifteen minutes. And she asked me something to the tune of whether I had any other bright ideas about what I might do if I left law school. I didn't.

Needless to say, I didn't feel so great after that meeting, but I also didn't have any idea of what I would do if I quit and left law school. So I decided to stay and stick it out, and things did get better. It certainly got much better after I bought a decent winter coat and about the same time, learned from the building super that heating charges were included in my rent. I therefore cranked the thermostat up to a balmy eighty-two degrees, put on my University of Hawaii rainbows shorts, and hit the books. Ultimately I found my way in law school, made some great friends whom I still have today, and ended up doing pretty well—certainly well enough to have some great opportunities after graduation.

But my career path has been a somewhat bumpy road in that I was never a hundred percent certain of exactly what it was I wanted to achieve with the skills I obtained in law school. It was also hard for me to learn how to be the captain of my own ship. Instead, I tended to team up with the loud or egomaniacal generals on the front lines and be a good soldier in the background. As a result, I had achieved success in that I earned a good living, had paid off all my student loans in the time allotted, and owned some real estate—but I was pretty unhappy. There were many fits and starts before I finally realized that what I really wanted to do was work part-time as a lawyer on my own with some clients I really liked, and use the remaining time to be with my family and to write. Many thought I was crazy to walk away from a good job, but walk away I did, and it was the very best thing I ever did. Having more time with my family has been a blessing with no end, and having the freedom to write something other than commercial documents has opened up a whole new world for me. I may never make as much money as when I worked full-time as a lawyer, and honestly, I couldn't care less, as I truly believe that one should never equate money with real success. We all know that the world abounds with big-money-makers who are miserable failures as human beings. In my mind, what counts most about success is how it is achieved.

There are some people who know from a very early age exactly what they want to do when they mature. They are happy on the road to their goal, and achieve the goal with the focus of one who is certain, clear and confident in his or her convictions. They are happy as clams when they reach their goal, and content as they cruise down the career path of their professional aspirations. My husband is one of those incredibly lucky people. He simply loves his work, and always has. He is very good at it, is well-respected in his field by both colleagues and opponents, and, by all standards, is a very successful man. That kind of singular certainty and focus can make people with lesser degrees of career conviction quite jealous at the ease of his career path's journey. Even, or especially, his wife! But of course I am delighted to have a spouse who in turn is so happy and satisfied by his career. Truthfully, it really is his life's calling and it is especially gratifying to bear witness to one who has reached the professional goals he set for himself when he was very young. While we often miss him as he spends long hours away from our family marching on to fulfill his dream, I know that every morning when he bounds out of bed at the crack of dawn, raring to get to work, he is a happy and successful man.

His consistent happiness, good nature and resulting success continued to inspire me to succeed in finding mine. Success has come to me finally, as I now love what I do. All of the component parts serve their purpose and finally fit together and fit well. That's pretty happy-making.

23

You are bound to your family of origin by DNA and, one hopes, the experience of time and love. If not, then embrace your family of choice even closer to your heart.

Two popular television shows of my youth, *Ozzie and Harriet* and *Father Knows Best,* portrayed television writers' fantasies of family life during that period. Though as everyone with a pulse knows, even intact families not beset by divorce, financial ruin, illness or other things often fell far short in reality of the ideal family's lofty portrayals on-screen. Those portrayals, while amusing in the black-and-white abstract of television, were an impossible standard in the living color of real-life practice. And sorry, my dear Harriet, there isn't a cake recipe in the free world that can be thought up, shopped for, hand-mixed, baked, and served up on good china in a half-hour, all the while the baker is fashionable dressed and perfectly coiffed. But nice try just the same.

The truth, of course, is that no family is perfect, no matter what it looks like to those on the outside staring into our family window – perfection simply cannot be achieved when mere mortals and the genuine messiness of real life are involved. One hopes, though, that as you mature you can learn to accept those in your family of origin with all of the compassion and understanding necessary in order to keep the peace among you, not to mention to preserve your sanity. Sometimes though, no matter what you do or say, or try to do or say, you fall short, even painfully short, and you simply cannot do it. Then you are left with what appears to be a Hobson's choice: continue the same path while feeling that you are not being true to yourself or your personal experience, or worse, being abused in some manner; or disengage altogether, resulting in a painful though temporary sense of limb amputation. It is not a choice for the faint of heart, but it is a choice which must be made, one way or the other, and then lived with.

I had what was considered at the time a somewhat unusual family story. Following my parents' divorce when I was nine, I was then raised by my single, hard-working mother. That was not so unusual, but what came before was. Prior to her marriage to my father, she had been married in Israel at eighteen, and by nineteen was the mother of an infant son. When she was twenty-one, she learned that her young husband had taken up with another woman. By the time she was twenty-two, she was divorced and had custody of her son. Then the opportunity arose for her to come to the U.S. with her work. By then her former husband had remarried. The arrangement my mother and her first husband made was that their son would live with him and his new wife for a couple of months, until my mother got settled in the U.S. At that time she would send for her son to join her. It was a fairly avant-garde arrangement in somewhat unusual circumstances given the international element, but as my mother would later describe it to me, she and her first husband were on decent terms. Or so she had thought.

Ten weeks after making this arrangement with her former husband, now settled in New York and working at the Israeli Consulate General, my mother sent for her son as they had agreed. That was when her personal Armageddon commenced. She learned that, contrary to the agreement they had made, and all semblance of sanity, her son was not living with her first husband and his new wife, but had been inexplicably placed by his father in an orphanage! Telegrams flew, family members got involved, embassy letters were sent, but as my mother recalled, it was as if she had stepped into a bureaucratic, hellish, Middle-Eastern twilight zone. She could not get her son out of the orphanage to save her life. She was despondent and beside herself. Her son remained at that orphanage for three long years—then, as soon as it appeared that she was close to success in finally getting him sent to her in the U.S., without warning or explanation, her first husband got their son out of the orphanage and brought him to live with him, his wife and their two young children. Then he unilaterally decided and made clear that he would never send their son to the U.S., not even for a visit.

My mother made dozens of trips to Israel over the years to attempt to repair the damage inflicted and to forge a relationship with her first-born child. Access to her son was virtually non-existent when he was at the orphanage, and limited while he was living with his father's family—and in both instances, he had been fed a steady diet of revisionist history, outright lies and lame half truths. To this day, no one knows what, precisely, my half-brother was told by those running the orphanage at the time. He was lucky, he would tell me years later, in that his step-mother was kind to him while he lived with her and his father, although he readily admitted that he never at any point in his life had a good relationship with the latter—a man he described as a simple, angry, and an inherently mean-spirited person.

I first met my half-brother when I was fifteen and he was twenty-six. He was in medical school in Italy by then and nearly finished, and was on his first trip to the U.S. He had been spoken of in our home ever since my earliest childhood memories. He occupied an odd place in my consciousness, in the way that happens when one hears about someone allegedly close by gene-pool standards, yet who is inexplicably in absentia and thus completely out of sight and reach. Meeting him for the first time was simultaneously a long-awaited yet unnerving experience. He was smart and, in graduate school, handsome, fluent in several languages, and already very well-traveled. I was an obnoxious, unruly and insecure American teenager.

His first language was Hebrew, and he was, of course, able to speak easily and with perfect grammatical correctness to our mother in their native language. We didn't share a common first language; we didn't even share a common country! So how on earth was it possible that we were at all related? He had no clue what to make of me or what to talk to me about. And I think that amused him, since he always said he could talk to a door hinge and get it to respond. No doubt he would have made a truly great lawyer, if only he had learned to type. So to bridge the gap, he did what any self respecting person in our ethnic gene pool did – he talked about food, specifically pizza, since he'd spent the preceding years in Italy. Now that was a subject I knew something about.

In the years which followed, we forged an unlikely alliance which can sometimes transpire between two people of incredibly disparate backgrounds. When I became a young adult, in an attempt to make up for lost time, we ended up traveling abroad several times to various countries when school schedules and circumstances permitted. During one such trip, to Asia, he met a lovely woman who would, a few years later, become his wife and the mother of his children. My connection to him was that of the sibling I never had; but since he already had two half-siblings with whom he had grown up, his connection to me was through the mother he never had.

There was certainly conflict over the years, most of which concerned our different understandings and perceptions of our mother. My mission in life, therefore, became to get him to see what an amazing person she was and how selfless she had been with me over the years. His early experience, of course, was wholly different, and, he admitted, stuck in the eyes of a young child summarily dumped without explanation like an unwanted piece of garbage into an awful Dickensian like orphanage, and then brainwashed by his father and his father's family. As the years went on, my utterly relentless mission continued unabated. This included paper chases, fact-finding trips to Israel, and lengthy interviews with family members involved with the situation at the time. After being presented with all that I had uncovered, he seemed to start to see and to appreciate our mother's many qualities, and the enormous obstacles she had faced in the late 1950s and early 1960s, with the Israeli bureaucratic nightmare and draconian state of family law there at the time. He also seemed to begin to lay to rest some of the long-standing lies he had been force-fed for so long.

During the period when our mother was terminally ill and I was caring for her at home in Hawaii, he came to the U.S. for a couple of weeks. It was quite surreal. He acted as though it were any other visit, not really discussing the illness or her terminal state, both somewhat odd, given that he was by then a physician. He never discussed the past with her, never genuinely forgave her, and when he left the islands that last time, when he knew the end was near, he never said goodbye. It was a terribly bitter pill for me. I can only imagine what it must have been for our mother. Though, true to my mother's character, she didn't discuss with me what must have felt like a thirty-year-old continuing crack in her heart.

Despite my deep sadness about how he handled the end, my half-brother and I maintained a quite cordial relationship for many years. We spoke fairly often by phone, sent long letters from wherever on the planet we were, and visited as regularly as we could, given our busy practices and young families situated on different continents.

As the years went on, though, it seemed that bit by bit, the glue which had held our relationship together had simply disintegrated. It was not something as simple as time or distance. Even though we were both busy, we were both better-placed than most to control our schedules, and we were both people who lived for jet fuel. After a while I started to think that it was something as simple as the mental aging process and how that interacts over the long-term with the presence of one's long-standing unresolved conflicts. Without exception, every single time we had spoken or spent time together during the five years before our relationship ended, he would say very negative things, often in public, about our mother—things which I knew for a fact were untrue. It was as if the long journey we had gone on up to that point had ceased to exist; all that we had learned had been forgotten in the years since our mother's death. These continuing instances were very painful for me. It was not that I couldn't bear to hear his pain, which I knew was still there, unresolved and an ever-present plunging dagger in his otherwise-good heart. I did listen with compassion and did so relentlessly. But it seemed as though speaking ill of the dead became the only way he could discuss our family history in any manner, even if what he spoke about was not based on his own experience or was, indeed, contrary to the facts that those around him knew.

So I tried another tactic: to leave our mother out of all of our conversations. However, our mother was our only real familial tether, as we didn't have the many years of time and experience that most siblings or family members share. As a result, the white elephant always seemed to be lurking just around the corner. While this was plainly uncomfortable for me, I was willing to keep the white elephant at bay in order to maintain what we had created, however tenuous it had become. I had no family members living in the U.S. and precious few abroad; I just didn't feel I could psychologically afford to excommunicate him altogether. I believed I needed someone connected to my family of origin in order to make sense of my current ride in life. I needed someone who had borne witness to the most important part of my past. But he couldn't or wouldn't control the white elephant. Since he couldn't talk about it in any meaningful way, he did what many people do when their discomfort escalates—he made endless streams of lame and often very hurtful jokes about our mother to deflect his own pain. This was utterly unbearable for me.

During my last visit, we were eating lunch at a seaside restaurant in old Yaffo with a whole group of his friends and two of his cousins. One acquaintance at the table questioned him, wondering how it came to pass that he was clearly a native speaker of Hebrew, while I spoke with an amalgam, mostly French accent – a very typical question we often had to field. Instead of answering the question directly and as simply and straightforwardly as possible, he instead made a slew of absurd jokes about our mother. Everyone went silent with the perplexed looks of those who have become well-aware that they have just stepped into a minefield with about five seconds to explosion.

The next day, I pleaded with him to stop, as I simply could no longer tolerate this hurtful disparagement of the loving woman who raised me alone in the U.S., who gave me every possible opportunity, and who did right by me at every turn during the time I had her in my life. I told him that these outbursts served to damage me and what was left of the memories of my mother and the experience of my childhood. He said that I could never understand what he went through and never would. This was, of course, true, I told him. However, that didn't change where we were today. She's gone and we are not, I told him. It was my feeling that we should preserve what we had as her legacy, and our gift to our own children on two continents. It was the night before I was to return to the U.S., and it was two o'clock in the morning. He said I would never be capable of understanding his inherent jealousy of me, since I had our mother all to myself and he had a pleasant-enough, though very marginal substitute. And there it was, finally out in the open. He was nearly sixty-years-old and I was then forty-seven. He never said goodbye to me that night, even though I was staying in his home. The next morning I took a cab to the airport at five a.m. for my early morning departure. I knew we would never speak again. And we haven't.

It's been three years since that night. I am still close to his former wife of nearly twenty years, and my teenaged daughter still speaks regularly to her only cousins, their now-young-adult sons who live in Europe. I've of course thought about our odd story a thousand different ways from Tuesday. And I'm sure my husband often wishes he had ready access to a wifely mute button, as I've talked about this topic so much in the intervening years. I truly wish the outcome had been different. I wish this in an intensely yearning and ravenously hungry way that only one with so few relatives anywhere, and with none in her own country, can. However, all the wishing in the world isn't going to change the outcome. I have finally come to a place where I understand that I cannot blame my half-brother for his inability to separate me from the terrible and outrageous tragedy that befell him when he was so young and most vulnerable. But I also know the truth that I uncovered and that I shared with him. It may not have been a truth that he was able to accept or even hear, since he had been operating from a deeply engraved book of falsehoods, misconceptions and half-truths for so many years. They provided him with the psychological scabs that he needed in order to allow some modicum of healing of the deep and lasting wounds he endured. And this became his modus operandi for survival. In choosing to let go of something that was so vitally important to me, I truly felt that I had cut off a necessary limb of my own—the limb which connected me to a timeless sense of family and shared history, no matter how bizarre it was and regardless of how many time zones it crossed. It was my birthright and I desperately wanted it, but I had to let go because to keep it would have stolen away from me the memory of all that was good about my own childhood and history.

I have also found over the years that your family of choice – the people whom you have added to your inner circle and to your family life—cannot only save you, but can actually be the family you didn't have in the obvious absence of the *Ozzie and Harriet* myth. I was lucky—there were two families in our small neighborhood in Hawaii that made sure I was at either one or the other of their homes on Christmas breaks for the five years following my mother's passing. There were law school classmates' families who "adopted" me for Thanksgiving and Easter during law school, and who vociferously cheered me on as I crossed to stage to receive my law degree at graduation. When I returned to Hawaii to practice, there was another dear friend whose father learned that I was about to buy a car and finance it. He showed up at the dealership unannounced and paid for the car in cash, telling me that "car loans were incredibly stupid." He then told me that I could pay him back when I could, but there would be no interest, except that I had to promise to join them regularly for Sunday dinners. If that's not real family, then I certainly don't know what is. While there was a dearth of genetic family members at my wedding, it was chock-full of friends who had traveled far and wide to share in the celebration. And while I had no people to whom I was linked by DNA at the hospital when my daughter was born, my mailman threatened to quit his job every day for the week after I got home from the hospital, he was burdened with the delivery of so many gifts from far-away friends.

Family is bestowed upon you by accident of birth, or acquired by choice. I hope that time and circumstance will allow you the luxury of having both. Your genetic compatriots may have shared a childhood with you, and likewise have a long thread of time and experiences and parental influences to carry you onward as you traverse and enjoy adulthood. But if, because of circumstances, you do not get a family at birth which is sustainable for whatever reason, you can love and nurture your family of choice and hold them close and hug them tighter. Very often in this life, the family you yourself choose will be there for you with a full heart and open arms. And they'll be the ones cheering you on for the duration.

24

Some friends will turn out to be more significant in your life than you ever thought imaginable or possible. Lucky you.

Sophie, my dearest friend in the world, died in Paris on July 30, 2003 when she was fifty-seven. Sophie heartily embraced the best of both the old and the new French worlds with style, panache and charm. She embodied the epitome of the "new" Frenchwoman, yet at the same time fiercely held onto some old and quirky French habits.

Sophie married young and had two children in fairly short order. When the children were four and six, she learned her husband was having a continuing affair with a neighbor, though he came home every evening for family dinners and otherwise kept up with his familial obligations. Most Frenchwomen at that time would have stayed firmly put, a la Mme. Mitterand, but not Sophie. In a move that prompted much outrage in her extended family and social circle, she promptly moved out and divorced her husband. In another odd-for-the-times maneuver, she moved to a house nearby his, so the children would have regular access to their father. Sophie then decided to start a business to position herself better to support herself and her children for the long term. She started a commercial office building cleaning service, though she knew virtually nothing about real estate and even less about cleaning. She hired recent immigrants from Portugal and Brazil, and then Sri Lanka, Senegal and India, not out of any sense of exploitation, she explained, but simply because she said, "the French never applied for these jobs." What started out as a small business with three teams of four employees each rapidly grew to a few hundred. The business was very successful, not just because the company provided excellent service to its commercial clients, but because her employees were devoted to her in a manner normally reserved for highly revered clergy. Sophie was not just the owner of the company and her employees' boss, she was their friend, confidante, substitute mom, French bureaucracy decipherer *par excellence*, political consultant, alternate dispute mediator, social-status mocker and all-around jokester. She also had a heart that ran as long and as wide as the Seine. Sophie's employees simply loved her.

Sophie had a circle of international friends that would make most diplomats blanche. And dinners *chez* Sophie were often a mix of French, Portuguese, Spanish, Hindi, Urdu and whatever other language and food du jour Sophie's newest friends brought with them—but besides me, there was never American and no English. Sophie learned the basic words in most of the languages of her friends, but I could never, ever get her to try to master even the most basic English other than "Good Morning" or "Thank you." She would simply giggle her deep, throaty laugh and say *"Mais pour quoi? J'ai toi dans ma vie et donc ce n'est pas du tout necessaire."* "But why? I have you in my life and so it's not at all necessary." At this I would roll my eyes with a grin and she would, in typical French fashion, pour another glass of red wine and light up yet another cigarette.

I first met Sophie at the opening of a restaurant of a mutual acquaintance on the Left Bank. I was working for an American law firm, and had stopped by for a quick drink after work. Again, in atypical French fashion, about fifteen minutes into our conversation, she invited me to her country home for brunch the following weekend. As I was leaving the restaurant that evening, Sophie told me to she was looking forward to my visit, and to please bring two kilos of carrots. A couple of days later I called the owner of the restaurant where we met and asked him about the odd carrot request. He started laughing, and told me under no circumstances should I arrive *chez* Sophie's without the requested vegetables, and then promptly hung up.

The following weekend I arrived, dutifully carrying two kilos of carrots, but feeling a bit foolish. After all, what person on earth could need so many carrots for a Sunday brunch? At Sophie's country home, I met her children, her granddaughter and her two prized stallions—hence the carrots. Later on she said with a wink that she asked me to bring the carrots because while she knew her friends and family would fall in love with me, she had to be absolutely sure that her stallions would. And as they loved nothing more than fresh carrots, they would simply have no choice but to love me. That was vintage Sophie, combining the sublime with the ridiculous and then delivering it with a hearty laugh, a broad smile and a kiss on both cheeks. Over the ensuing months and years, I understood what her employees and other friends well knew: that Sophie was simply an utterly remarkable woman, generous to a fault, completely devoid of class-consciousness and without a racist or bigoted bone in her petite 5'2" body. She was, without a doubt, simply one of the most decent human beings who ever graced the planet.

A year later, when the owner of the apartment I was renting would not renew my lease, since he had family returning to France, I was in the middle of a massive work project with no time to spare, much less to search out new lodgings. Sophie not only found me a perfect apartment, but had some of her employees move my belongings while I was in the U.S. for a week, and then fully stocked the kitchen for my return. Months later, when I was going on and on about a recent breakup while she was driving me back to my apartment following dinner, she offered to stay over and keep me company even though she knew it meant she would be sleeping on the floor, so we could have breakfast together. Years later, when I was living in the U.S. and going through a particularly rough patch with the Surgeon Who Wasn't, she would set her alarm to wake up in the middle of the night so that she could call me at a decent hour for a lengthy conversation and to make sure I was doing okay. And in June of 2003, when my daughter and I arrived in Paris for the summer and Sophie was in the hospital undergoing chemotherapy, unbeknownst to me, she somehow arranged for a furnished apartment for us near the Luxembourg Gardens. And of course the kitchen was fully stocked, down to my daughter's favorite yogurt.

We stayed in the apartment that summer, and Sophie and I talked incessantly. She never let on just how ill she was, and she and her family were positive and upbeat about her medical care. By late July she seemed to be doing better. Another friend had invited me to the countryside for a couple of days and Sophie urged me to go and escape the Parisian heat. As I was getting ready to return to Paris, I was called by her son and told that Sophie had passed away peacefully in her sleep.

There are moments in life when you are confronted by an event that, no matter how hard you try, simply will not register into your stream of consciousness. This was one such moment. It just wasn't possible. I had just left Paris two days before, and Sophie was doing so much better. I simply could not imagine life without my dear Sophie, the multifaceted woman who had become not just my best friend in the world, but the older sister I never had. I had lost my father as a consequence of his demons and my parents' divorce, grew up without my only brother, then lost my mother and my grandparents in my early twenties, and now my Sophie. It was nearly more than I could bear. I got back to Paris as quickly as I could, with a swollen, tear-stained face and a breaking heart.

Sophie's funeral, in August of 2003, occurred during one of the worst heat waves in France's history, and the average temperature in Paris was hovering at 104 degrees. In a compact city with virtually no air conditioning, it was unbearable, and several thousand Parisians—mostly elderly people—perished that summer from heat exposure. The collective national mourning seemed to match my own. The friend in whose restaurant Sophie and I met years before, and another dear mutual friend who owned a farm in Southern France, both arrived at the same time at my apartment. Together we drove from central Paris to a suburb about ninety minutes away, where the funeral home and crematorium were located. It was only when we arrived that I understand why this place so far away had been chosen. It was an utterly surreal event—not only due to the choking heat, but because there were at least 600 people present, many of whom wore the traditional clothing of the countries from which they had originally hailed. There were entire families in flowing robes and colorful skirts, western suits and dresses, as well as veritable mountains of flowers, and massive amounts of burning incense. I have never seen so many distraught people in one place in my life, and never have I seen so many tears. The friend from Southern France said shortly after we got out of the car that the scene appeared to him as if a greatly beloved parish priest had died, so evident and so intense was the collective grief. As the service ended and the crowd headed toward the crematorium, I nearly passed out from my overwhelming sadness, the massive crowd, the stifling heat and the burning incense. And given how many relatives of mine had perished in crematoria in the next country over, I simply could not go on. I leaned on my friend, and we started to walk away. As we headed toward the car, we saw a group of Sophie's Brazilian friends whom I had met several times at her country home. With tears in his eyes, the most macho of the group said to me, "There will never, ever be another Sophie." That was the simple truth. I could not bring myself to go back to the Paris apartment, so my friend invited us to his family farm in the South of France. There, with his wife and their children and their horses, a noisy donkey and a few dozen chickens scurrying about, we stayed up late into the nights, drinking wine from their cave and telling remarkable and touching Sophie stories that we had amassed over the years. As that week came to a close, we all had accumulated a great reservoir of lessons and love to hold on to in order to carry on.

On my desk I keep a large photo of a widely smiling Sophie feeding carrots to her beloved stallions at her country home with her granddaughter and my daughter laughing in the foreground. I am thus reminded daily of her generosity of spirit, her grace and her enormously oversized heart. Sophie was so much more than a great friend, so much more than the sister I never had. Sophie was a constant reminder to be open to experiencing life on its own terms, to reach out to those you may never otherwise have the good fortune to know—and above all, to share its largesse. From a chance meeting at a small French bistro came into my life a beacon of love, acceptance and the true meaning of family, regardless of race, language or religion. I will hold onto that for the rest of my life. There may indeed never, ever be another Sophie, but the power and significance of her lessons and her love live on and continue to touch me in ways I never thought possible or imaginable. Lucky me. And in the refrigerator of my life, there shall always be two kilos of fresh carrots.

25

Keep things in perspective. Blisters do not require chemo.

Keeping problems, even the really annoying ones, which beset us during the ordinary course of our lives in their proper perspective is not just a critically important lesson. It is a lesson which we must constantly relearn on a regular and continuing basis. Perspective can keep you sane and even make you a happier person. Being happy doesn't mean that everything is perfect in life; it means that you decide to see beyond the imperfections. On the other hand, losing sight of what is really important in life is a crazy-making joy thief. And let's face it—who couldn't use a little bit more joy in their lives?

One of my dearest friends in the world is a sixty-seven-year-old attorney on the opposite coast. He is part brilliant mentor, part kindly uncle, part sage, all devoted friend and the best possible full-time moral compass. I will never forget how he literally yelped in delight following my engagement when I asked him to fly across the country to walk me down the aisle. This man has a heart substantially larger than the state of Texas. We e-mail like fiends, often ten times in one day if we're really on a roll, and talk regularly, since often we simply need to hear each other's voice in order to make sure that all is right in the world. He has children and grandchildren who are far luckier than lottery winners to have the privilege of calling him Dad and Gramps.

In early 2004, his beloved cousin Judy died after a terrible battle with breast cancer. Her young adult daughters, his nieces, decided to participate in the three-day, sixty-mile walk held by the Susan B. Komen Foundation to raise money for breast cancer research. He then decided there was no better way to honor his beloved cousin than to walk in her honor with her daughters and raise money for a cure. And that's how it began.

Since then, my friend has participated in twelve of those sixty-mile walks in several cities across the country, clocking 750 race miles and literally thousands of training miles. He has also singlehandedly raised over a $150,000 dollars for breast-cancer research. What better way to cope with grief and honor a loved one than that? My friend proudly wears his pink bracelet every single day, and a pink ribbon pin on his lapel, even to court. He can often be seen in the elevators of his Wall Street office building during lunchtime wearing a pink T-shirt and training shoes with hot pink laces as he steps out to walk, even in the often-unbearable heat of New York City summers. He has participated in various opening and closing ceremonies at these Komen walks, and has made innumerable and life-long friends along the way. He has raised money for other walking friends when they did not have enough sponsors or funds to participate. When he started walking, only two percent of walkers were men. Now he boasts that nine percent are men. He has walked and cried with his fellow walkers, many of whom are survivors or relatives of survivors or relatives of unlucky ones who didn't survive. He has then walked on and on and then cried some more.

Over the years, he has shared with his many friends and colleagues photographs and heartfelt essays following each of these three-day walks, describing his incredible experiences and the many friends he has made on his "Kill the Beast" missions. These photographs and often heartbreaking essays have become for me a continuous and continuing reminder to consistently recalibrate my own perspective about the problems which life often presents.

The vast majority of the everyday stuff we must deal with or which is thrown at us when we're busy doing something else is, for all intents and purposes, really just a blister. To be sure, sometimes the problem is an annoyance akin to a painful blister on the heel of your foot that hurts you with every single step you take until it heals. Other times, the problem may be more severe, so that it feels like a whole cluster of blood blisters on the sole of your foot that practically brings you to your knees at the mere thought of taking a step. But step you most certainly must, because the proverbial show must go on. There are things you must accomplish, places you must go and people who are depending on you who just really can't be concerned with your blisters, no matter how badly they make you limp or how much of a personal drag they are to you. And above all, remember the lesson of my best friend's beloved cousin, which should be a permanent mantra for better and happier living: "Keep your perspective. Blisters don't need chemo." So step up, step out and walk on. And on and on. There will probably be band-aids just around the corner.

26

Sometimes you really just need a good night's sleep. Good night, and sweet dreams.

Even Wall Streeters who work insanely long hours will tell you that nobody ever made a good financial decision when tired. If that is true, and I believe it to be so, how on earth can one expect to make a good emotional decision when tired? It just can't be done. And frankly, you shouldn't even try. Arthur Schopenhauer, the pessimistic 19th century German philosopher, once said, "Sleep is the interest we have to pay on the capital which is called in at death; and the higher the rate of interest and the more regularly it is paid, the further the date of redemption is postponed." I'm not so sure about the pessimistic capital call, but we all do need a really good night's sleep.

A good night's sleep, with the renewed sense of clarity and calm it provides, is critical to our thought process and the ability to make sound decisions; however, good-quality rest is often very difficult to come by. Each of us has a minimal sleep requirement that we must make every evening in order to keep us functioning at our best. If we don't get what we need, the result is a sleep debt. The usual thieves of high-stress, an unbalanced or poor diet, and an overindulgence in caffeine, of course, add to our dearth of sound sleep. And regular insomnia, whether the type that doesn't allow you to fall asleep in the first place or the type that wakes you up raring to go at the ungodly hour of three a.m., is enough to bring you to your knees. The lack of good, sound sleep simply cannot be maintained over the long term, as both productivity and mood will be negatively altered.

Assuming there isn't something physiologically amiss which is causing your slumber to be stolen from you, you must figure out, by trial and error if necessary, what it is that is causing the sleep robber to prey on your bed.

I remember with such fondness my teenage years and the ability to sleep well into the afternoon on the weekends with ease and finally waking up with only my body clock as the internal alarm. There was nothing more utterly delicious. Even in college, I recall sleeping until noon after a late night studying or working. The ability to sleep deeply and for long hours with such reckless abandon disappeared so quietly and so completely, that I can't actually remember when it departed—though I imagine it must have happened at some point between my last set of college finals and the onset of parenting.

No matter how many well-meaning friends, colleagues or neighbors you have with children, how much you read on the subject or how many stories you may have heard, you will simply never believe or be prepared for the sleep deprivation that comes with having a newborn. It's completely unfathomable. No one spoke the truth on the subject any better than Leo J. Burke, who said, "People who say they sleep like a baby probably don't have one." By the time our daughter was three months old, the sleep deprivation had nearly driven me insane. I simply was unable to think straight. And I don't need a full eight hours of sleep to function well; five is just fine. It wasn't just the feedings every few hours during the night, though that certainly nearly did me in. It was also that during the days when I was at home, I didn't heed the cardinal rule of going to sleep every time the baby did. Instead, I ran around like a chicken with its head cut off trying to make headway on the never-ending to-do list and trying to get some work done in between. Until one day I put the dogs' dinner in their bowls and, for reasons which still remain a mystery, promptly put the dogs bowls in the oven—which in my slumber-challenged state, I had, thankfully forgotten to turn on. When my husband got home later that evening he said aloud that the dogs

165

were acting strange, a bit hyper, as if they hadn't been fed. These dogs needed nothing to be a bit hyper, I assured him, they were just born that way. I went to the refrigerator to get the rotisserie chicken I had bought earlier in the day so I could warm it for his dinner, but it wasn't there. What happened, I tried to think in my sleep-deprived haze? Did the chicken get into a beef with the cold cuts in the deli drawer and then get so mad that it got up and stormed out of my kitchen? Like a semi-conscious maniac, I took everything out of both the refrigerator and freezer. No luck. I then started opening and shutting every cabinet and drawer in the kitchen until, finally, I opened the pantry containing the canned dog food and kibble. And right there, next to a mountain of Alpo, sat a lonely, foil-covered, spoiling chicken. The chicken went into the trash, the dogs finally got their belated dinner, we ordered in Chinese food, and from that day forward, I napped every time the baby did. I also think my husband never quite looked at chicken in exactly the same way after that either.

Sleep deprivation aside, I would never, ever advocate going to bed angry, whether it stems from an upsetting work-related issue or family-related problem that needs to be worked through. That said, sometimes you just need to sleep in order to work things through to a successful resolution. I can't count the number of times I've gone to sleep with a problem that seemed insurmountable or frustrating beyond measure, only to wake up and miraculously come up with several potential solutions to the problem which was, only five or six hours before, making me crazy. This doesn't always work, of course, but for me it usually does. John Steinbeck said it succinctly when he wrote, "It is a common experience that a problem difficult at night is resolved in the morning after the committee of sleep has worked on it."

How comforting it is to think that when I have a problem, an entire committee is hard at work on it while I sleep in order to solve it for me! If only that were the case. Actually, the committee may not be solving it for me, but *with* me. By "committee," I am referring to the dream state. It's a time when so many bits of factual information that come at you during the day, which never enter your consciousness while awake, arrive (often in Technicolor) during the rapid-eye-movement phase of sleep to guide you through an often-random, sometimes kaleidoscopic amalgam that assists you in sorting things out when you arise. I cannot discount the role that dreams can often play in either understanding certain problems or facilitating their resolution. With some regularity, my husband and I play the dream post-mortem over our morning coffee (that is, after the dogs have been fed; no chickens in sight). It is often remarkable how sometimes odd, ill-fitting pieces can come together and aid in the provision of clarity. It has often been the case that he is better at reading the importance of some of my dreams than I am and vice-versa.

To make the best possible decisions, you need to be well rested. All of us, at one time or another, have difficulties getting to or staying asleep. If that's the case, do what you can to figure out the cause, and attempt to correct it. Try and get at least the minimum amount of sleep that you need to feel your best, so that you will be able to do your best and likewise be your best. And if you are having a rough patch, for whatever reason, postpone when possible making any big or life-altering decisions. When the babies finally fall asleep, hopefully with a dry diaper, join them as often as possible. And if you find an erstwhile chicken in a cabinet with the Alpo, it really is high time to take a well-deserved nap. Sleep well, and sweet dreams.

27

Prejudice is the natural child of shallow thoughts. Delve deeper.

Let's face it; it is far easier to think inside the box into which we are either born or educated, or in which we are comfortable, than it is to think outside that box or personal comfort zone. Hawaii, where I spent my formative years, has such a unique political, economic and social history that the unintended result turned out to be quite an incredible social experiment with a melting pot of people that really respects the various cultural backgrounds of its constituent parts. That said, Hawaii is not a racial panacea, but it is certainly as close to it as I've ever seen anywhere in the world. After all, how easy is it to have racial prejudices in a place where most people can boast several very different ethnicities in their own family trees? At any random gathering of people, personal or professional, you can talk to an Asian person with a Western last name and vice-versa, with every possible amalgam imaginable in between. I recall one friend describing his ethnic background to another, saying, "I'm Hawaiian, Chinese, Filipino, Portuguese, French and Scottish, but that's just on my mom's side." That's pretty much par for the course in Hawaii.

Hawaii, though, is a fairly small island state and, given its unusual history, it would be difficult to replicate its societal experiment in an average American metropolis. On the other hand, continuing migration to American shores from other regions of the world poses even bigger challenges as global distances have become smaller, economic differences wider, and assimilation of certain groups more difficult in places where diversity is rarer. It thus makes it even more important to remember Walt Whitman's wise words: "We are a country of equal daughters and equal sons...all alike endear'd." Of course, this is easier said than done, and in some ways, it is more difficult for many to keep this concept of this nation's historical mandate in the forefront of our social existence in a post-9/11 world. But we must. It is part and parcel of our American social fabric and the very basis of its ideals. So much of what is wonderful about America is, of course, that we have been and, I hope, will always remain, a country of inclusion.

The more opportunities you have to live around different kinds of people, the better-prepared and equipped you are to live in this complex and colorful world and the more able you are to be open to the differences that other people and cultures possess. This opportunity does not necessarily have to be in Belarus or Mongolia or any other far-away place, given the nature of the melting pot that is America. However, very often we are better-able to open our hearts and minds to the requisite level of understanding necessary to those who are different from us when we are not in the cultural comfort zone of our home turf. Being in the minority in a particular place, or not understanding its differing language or culture, permits development of a capacity for the greatest possible understanding and its wonderful twin sister, empathy—provided the desire for these things is there. Reading certainly helps, and provides a baseline for understanding those differences. And I certainly am a voracious reader. But I do not believe books or lectures or policy statements can ever be substitutes for the visceral understanding you can gain by, for example, holding a foreign newborn in your arms or staring deep into the eyes of a person with whom you share nothing other than the bread you together break. Once the human divide is crossed, not only do the differences become less important, but you also start to realize how insignificant they really are. At our core, our needs as human beings are pretty much all the same regardless of where on the planet you hail from and what the cultural differences are. Once we understand this, it is much easier to think outside the box.

As prejudice is the natural-born child of shallow thoughts, I therefore suggest that you adopt a wider angle lens. Adopt a broader view so that you may delve further. You never know what you will learn. But whatever it is that you learn, it is more than you knew before. Prejudice is anathema to the very essence of what makes this country the great place it is, warts and all. While it is always easier to remain standing still in our comfort zone, the biggest rewards may come to you when you step outside that zone. And they will probably come when and where you least expect it.

28

Your fears are not your friends. Identify and face them, then kick them to the curb and carry on.

Sometimes it seems we carry our fears with us like some sort of blanket. And an insecurity blanket at that. Often the very thing which you fear the most in life may be exactly what you need to face head-on in order to grow. Or, indeed, to grow up.

In my late twenties, I had a lovely though fairly empty apartment, a new car and most of the yuppie trappings, but noticed that I didn't feel any more secure than when I was a struggling college student or a grad student with all hopes pinned on a bright future. Most of my friends were buying condominiums or small starter homes, but I couldn't bring myself to take the plunge. This was even more comical, since I was a real estate lawyer and knew all of the benefits of doing so. It was as if the shoemaker's daughter were going barefoot. I just couldn't do it, even though I knew every single reason and benefit to why *you* should.

After a while it became sort of a standing joke at my firm. One lawyer would routinely march into my office with newspaper ads circled in red ink, and another would have his wife the real estate broker call me regularly. Still no dice. It wasn't that I didn't want a place of my own; I did, but it was far too frightening even to contemplate. Even a small condominium was too much. The thought of committing myself on that scale just scared me to death. I was also afraid that buying a place on my own somehow sent a message to the world that I wanted to *be* alone. So I made a whole host of excuses to myself and to others and continued to pay exorbitant rent, never really settling in or making the place I was in feel like a home, since it wasn't mine, and enviously admiring my friends who were plunging into bricks and mortar.

About a year later, my colleague's wife called me and, practically out of breath, told me that a really great place had just become available in my price range and I should come quickly and take a look at it. Things were slow that afternoon at the office and I was a bit bored, and so I decided meet her and take a look. I called a friend of mine who liked to look at real estate, and off we went. It was true that the location was great and the place was perfect in every single respect. After we left, my friend was very excited about the place, and talking a mile a minute about its many virtues—so much so that I finally told him that if he liked the place so much *he* should buy it. He laughed and reminded me that he already owned a house. He then got serious and said, "Okay, what is your problem? You need to buy a place, and this is a great one. What is it precisely that you are afraid of?" I was really taken aback as I had never associated my inability to take the plunge of buying a house as having anything to do with real fear. I was just a sort of phobic about taking on that kind of debt. But the more I thought about it, the more I realized that I was chock-full of fear on the subject, and that the fear had zero to do with financing dirt, but that that covered up the real issues quite nicely, thank you very much. There was the usual and fairly acceptable fear about making a very big purchase, regardless of its usefulness; but this, of course, was the convenient cloud cover. Just underlying that was the fear that I really had to committing to being a lawyer and continuing to work in this profession in order to pay the mortgage. Then there was the fear that I wouldn't be able even to do that, and instead would end up an old lady in a parking lot, pushing a shopping cart overflowing with all of my worldly belongings. Finally, there was the fear that if I bought a place on my own and settled in, I was somehow signaling to the world a desire not to couple, and I would forever remain a single professional. Some of these were irrational fears, to be sure, but they were *my* fears, and they paralyzed me when it came to doing what was best for me and my future. I actually said to my friend, "But what if I can't pay the mortgage?" He laughed and reminded me of two things, both of which were true: one, I had never missed a rent payment in my entire life, even when I was living on chump change in college and law school; and two, the mortgage was less than the rent I had been paying for the past two years. This, he said, was "simple math." I always hated math.

I could not argue with my friend. He was dead right, and I knew it. I also recalled something I had read somewhere—that fear was an acronym for **f**alse **e**vidence **a**ppearing **r**eal. That was true too. I had never missed a rent payment once in my life. I had never bounced a check, and I could afford this place, even if I ultimately decided I didn't want to practice law but instead do something else with my training and skills. And even though the fear of the old lady pushing the stuffed shopping cart *felt* real as hell, it wasn't. And since when was making a financial investment that had the added collateral benefit of putting a roof over one's head a neon highway billboard for advertising terminal singledom?

I called the broker and made an offer. Back and forth the seller and I went, and we ultimately we came to an agreement. So I bought the place, though I confess that during the escrow period, I had heart palpitations while signing the Mount Everest of documents, and a couple of evenings of night sweats, thinking I had made a huge mistake. I also knew, though, that I had to move on in order to go on. Ralph Waldo Emerson said, "Do the thing you are afraid to do and the death of fear is certain." I can't say that the fear completely went away, but big progress was made. It turned out to be not only a great financial decision, but after a while it seemed somehow to quiet down the old lady—or at least relax her to the point where I didn't keep bumping into her blasted shopping cart and twisting my ankle every single time I thought about making a financial or career decision.

This also reminded me of a young Japanese woman I met on a boat from Algeciras on the coast of Spain near Gibraltar, heading to Tangiers. I was in law school, but traveling for a month in the summer with my former college roommate. Somewhere in southern Spain, a lone traveler from Indonesia had joined the two of us and continued with us on the boat to Morocco. On this crowded boat, really more of a people-moving ferry through the Straits of Gibraltar, the three of us spotted a slight Japanese woman who appeared to be traveling alone. She also, it turned out, didn't speak a single word of English. Or Spanish. Or French. Or Arabic. I struck up a conversation with her and told her about my host family in Japan and of some of my great experiences with them. She told me that she came from a small town in the very north of the country, had finished college and was about to start working, but wanted to take a big trip, as she was afraid that if she didn't go now, life would get in the way and she'd go back to her small town and miss the opportunity. This was her first trip abroad, and while she was having a great time seeing the world, it was a little surreal, as she hadn't spoken to anyone else in a number of days. She also said she was taking a lot of notes to make sure she didn't forget any of the places she went to or the sights she saw—the very bane of the solo traveler's experience. I remember thinking then that she was either completely nuts or the most courageous woman I had ever met to date. I decided it was the latter. While English or French or Spanish isn't of course spoken everywhere in the world, I've found that in many parts of the world you can usually find someone who knows at least a few words of one of those languages if you need help or run into some trouble. But the chances of finding a happenstance Japanese speaker meandering in Morocco or toiling in Tunisia if she ran into a traveler's travail? I wouldn't take that bet. And didn't. So I invited her to join our odd trio as we traveled through North Africa, and we became a still-odder quartet. We also had a really great time together.

Later Kumiko told me that getting on the plane by herself to start her journey was the scariest thing she had ever done—not because she was taking the journey alone, but because she was doing so without any English skills. She also believed that if she didn't do it then, she might never be able to, and she desperately wanted the experience so that she would feel calm returning to her small town and starting her life there after college. She knew what she needed to do and, while she was afraid, she did it anyway, she said, "to grow." That is most definitely courage.

Whatever your fear is, keep in mind that fear is a four-letter word and most certainly not your friend. Fear will stunt your growth and keep you from doing what is best for you. It can often take a long time to garner the courage to face those fears, especially since they often masquerade as long-time, comforting allies. When I finally closed escrow on that first condo, I opened a bottle of champagne with my friends and toasted Kumiko. She had shown me many moons earlier that real courage is the willingness to accept your fears and act anyway. And that's a really great lesson to hold onto. In any language.

29

Stop complaining and start doing.

A bit of complaining is often thought to be cleansing, akin to metaphorically scrubbing a pot before you rinse it off with cool, clean water, dry it, and put it back in the cupboard. And in small doses, in order to get something off your chest, complaining briefly can work wonders and make you feel better.

However, complaining simply for the sake of complaining does nothing other than to bore your audience. Often to tears. Complaining is not a permissible adjective, *unless* it is engaged in for the specific purpose of drafting a blueprint for change. And that blueprint needs to specify the fix with clarity, precision and conviction.

Last year, one of our sons was adjusting to university and dorm life in the mid-west. During a Skype call, he complained for what seemed like eternity that his former high school girlfriend, now in college on the east coast, called, texted or Skyped him incessantly at all hours of the day and night. Though he was still fond of her and conflicted over the breakup as only a teenager can be, he responded briefly to each of her continuous communications. It was driving him to distraction, and on and on he kvetched about it. After about twenty minutes of 'round and 'round Skype-kvetch, I could listen no longer and told him he had to *do* something about the problem if it bothered him. From my vantage point, he had two choices, I told him. He could gently and politely disengage from his old girlfriend, since, after all they had definitively broken up for good reasons and were now attending universities in different states. His other alternative was to stop complaining about her technological stalking if somehow he actually liked the distracting, slightly warped, attention from an old flame. He chose the former, thank goodness, and soon the annoying communications from her stopped completely.

Sometimes you need to bend a friend's, colleague's, spouse's or parent's ear about something which is bothering you. In moderation or with a clear purpose that's fine, cleansing, healthy, and usually does the trick in helping you move on. But remember that generalized kvetching is most certainly not a spectator sport. No one will ever want to purchase a ticket to a kvetching match, and there is no kvetching little league in preparation for the big leagues. There are no big leagues. And for very good reason.

Complaining without purpose also makes one unable to take advantage of the NOW principal. This admirable concept, which stands for "no opportunity wasted," was coined by Phil Keoghan, the popular emcee of the travel reality show *The Amazing Race*. Though obviously we can't necessarily take every single opportunity which comes our way in life, for a whole host of reasons, there are very many that we can. But you need to be able to see the opportunity, and then be able to grab it and run with it. Often a particularly wonderful opportunity may present itself even peripherally, but if you are so busy complaining about the problem *du jour,* you may miss an opportunity right under your nose which might resolve it. And to paraphrase David Shenk in *Slamming Gates,* constant complainers begin to look like malcontents who kvetch about the weather so much that they don't notice when the sun comes out.

Distraction is another useful tool to ward off the tendency to kvetch insufferably. This is particularly the case if the time during which you are distracted from your problem is spent helping other people. Aiding others, especially those who are less-fortunate in some way can often deliver remarkable gifts of insight and gratitude. And more often than not, your own gratitude is increased in direct proportion to the help you provide others. The added bonus of doing good works is that your own problems almost mysteriously diminish in comparison. This can, of course, be accomplished in a myriad of ways, either within your profession or outside of it. Indeed, going outside what you normally do day-to-day is yet another avenue by which to explore something different and provide help in a way that may change your own perspective about your problems and about life in general.

So remember—the next time your personal kvetch-o-meter starts to go into high overdrive, get out your drafting pencils and start planning your blueprint to change the circumstances. Make sure and keep your eyes peeled so that no opportunity is wasted. And if you are still feeling like kvetching, get busy helping someone less-fortunate. You may not be in a race, but you may truly be amazed at what happens.

30

No one in the world will ever love you like your mother did. That bus has already left the station.

This is very important, so let me just repeat it: No one in the world will ever love you like your mother did. Period, full stop, end of story. It is simply not possible, no matter how much your lover, spouse, or anyone else in the world cares about you. And they may really, truly and genuinely love you to pieces, beyond measure, and more than dark chocolate. But it is just not the same. A mother's love is exponentially off the charts on the Richter scale of emotive love. And I make zero distinction between biological mothers and adoptive mothers here. Indeed, one could easily argue that, given how difficult it is to adopt a child today, once adoptive mothers finally have their children, their love is fundamentally, by definition, equal to that of biological mothers.

There's no doubt that I was one of the lucky ones. I was told, and made to feel, by my mother every day of my childhood and youth that I was loved, special, and wanted. I also felt that she genuinely liked me as a person. When I was with my mother, I never felt she wanted to be elsewhere, even though I was well-aware of the personal and professional sacrifices she had made in her own life to assure that she would be there for me as much as humanly possible. This, of course, allowed me to go out in the world with a lot of confidence as I knew that, somehow, I would find my way. And this is even more important, since my parents died so young. If you think back to the hundreds of times you brought things home, what ever those things were—drawings, shells, dead sand crabs or butterflies—and the level of interest the vast majority of moms are able to conjure up, it's pretty darned remarkable. Day in and day out, mothers the world over do truly amazing things. And usually it's done while juggling a dozen other things at the same time.

I am also not downplaying the role of a father in a child's life, even though my own father did not participate in a positive or meaningful way for the vast majority of my childhood. Fathers, of course do all kinds of wonderful things all the time, including in some families raising the children virtually alone due to a wide variety of circumstances. What I am saying, however, is that I believe the contributions made to a child's life are different in the cases of mothers and fathers. Both parental influences are highly important, just completely different.

But let's face facts: no matter how wonderful your lover or spouse is, he or she will never love you in the same way as your mother did. No one actually can, and frankly, you will probably doom yourself to damnation if you expect it. The love we get from good parents is, without a doubt, the greatest gift in the universe. It also allows us to become good partners, and in turn to become good parents. But while we want our spouses simultaneously to be the president, treasurer and secretary of our personal fan clubs, they will often not think the dead sand crab you bring home is the coolest thing on planet earth, or the piece of art you made a Picasso look-a-like. Nor will they think that your hiccups are cute or that your burps smell like expensive perfume. What you can hope for in a good partnership—and with any luck get—is that your partner will listen to the tale of the dead sand crab with a modicum of actual interest, and look at the pretend Picasso and be genuinely happy that you are trying something new that appeals to you in some visceral way. As for the hiccups and burps in life, let's just hope for tolerant détente. If you get all of that, plus you really love your partner, then kiss him or her, as you are scoring a thousand in the batting cage of your love life. But to have or harbor the expectation that a partner will somehow manage to provide the level of unconditional love you were lucky enough to receive from your mother, or in some cases, your father, is simply not realistic, nor necessarily what you may really need from your partner. If you got that once in your life, when you were a child and needed it most, then you were one of the lucky ones. By pure genetic chance and circumstance, you got on the right bus and off you went to traverse the highway of life. If you didn't get it the first time around, from either or both of your parents, for whatever the reasons, you will need to come to terms with that loss however you are able. Even if it means finding a new, although different bus that only you can drive. But come to terms with it you must. To expect your spouse or partner to rise to that occasion is far too big a burden for any relationship to bear.

So tip your hat and celebrate all of the wonderful mothers and fathers out there. Acknowledge all of the unconditional love and support and the many kindnesses bestowed and sacrifices they made, so many of which go unnoticed and unappreciated when we are children and wholly self-absorbed. And if that bus has already left the station, and your parents are no longer there, then so be it. At least you managed to hitch a ride to the depot for another mode of transportation to carry on.

31

Loving a child changes everything. In ways you can't even begin to imagine.

People today often have the luxury of being able to "plan" their families. However, it's true that no matter how prepared you think you are for parenthood, how many books you've read, how many people you've talked to, how much money you've saved, or how many electrical outlets you've baby-proofed, you never truly are prepared for the monumental, life-altering changes that having a child brings. That is because they can't even be imagined, much less planned for. That there is untold magic is absolutely certain. I can say with complete conviction that the late afternoon of my daughter's birth bestowed upon me an experience that may be as close to divine intervention as I will ever experience in this lifetime.

There are, of course, the "usual" changes that parenting brings—lack of sleep resulting in near-terminal "blond" moments, an intense desire to take showers lasting more than twenty seconds, and the longing to wear for more than a minute a shirt not permanently stained with strange-colored baby barf, or worse. But you get used to all of that and far, far more, quite simply because there is nothing in the world like staring into your smiling child's face or hearing him or her giggle with reckless abandon. Nothing comes even remotely close.

When we become parents, we make changes to our lives, we make monumental sacrifices, we step and stretch very far outside of ourselves because we now are responsible for the health and welfare of another life. Sometimes we go farther than we ever thought humanly possible, which of course is why you hear stories of a mother moving an impossibly heavy object, like a car, that has pinned down her child. As any parent knows well, raising kids is not for the faint of heart. Often you need the loving heart of Mother Theresa, the patient grace of Mahatmas Ghandi, the delicate finesse of Dame Margot Fonteyn and the spinal column and strength of General George C. Patton. And often all at the same time. You also need an extremely large bucket of old-fashioned good luck.

Although the baby years are tough for many, mostly because of seemingly never-ending exhaustion, the true test of parenting a girl comes, of course, just following puberty. In my own parenting of a daughter, I have said with distinct regularity during this period (in addition to "Heaven help me," at least a hundred million times) that this must be some kind of cosmically karmic payback, as every single lousy thing I did or said to my own mother has now been done or said to me, seemingly tenfold. It's amazing how that happens—and our daughter is smart, a focused student and a really good kid. Even though you have some vague and foggy recollection that you were not the most wonderful teenager in the universe and said and did some hideous things, nothing in the world can quite prepare you for the very first time your kid utters those indelibly shocking words, "I hate you." Fortunately, in my case, it was said only once, and was followed immediately by a torrent of heartfelt tears, hugs, and apologies, but it was still shocking nonetheless. Though it did remind me of the time I said the exact same words to my own mother, followed in like form by a flood of tears, hugs, and apologies. But as a parent, you do get over it, since teenagers, especially teenage girls, often behave far worse and sometimes more bizarre than permanent residents of insane asylums. I have since decided that, more often than not, a daughter can only fully appreciate her mother when she has a daughter of her own or is over thirty, whichever happens to come first. Boys, of course, are far, far different during those teenage years, and I had to get used to years of unintelligible one-word grunts for answers (sounds that I had previously heard only from a crickety old washing machine), near-toxic body emanations, and jam packed refrigerator and freezers and pantries whose contents could be emptied out and consumed in under a minute flat.

As any parent can tell you, there are no guarantees in life when it comes to children. The reality is that we don't have very much control over the way children turn out. DNA makes many of the decisions for us well in advance, and the offspring possessing that DNA determine most of the balance. Some children let parents exert a great deal of influence, and others do not. Regardless, most blossom when we love them and give them the type of love they need. Worrying achieves precious little other than an abundance of sleepless nights and the early onset of gray hair and wrinkles. Parenting requires you to promise yourself that you will try your very best, set the best example possible, and then keep your fingers firmly crossed and hope for some good luck along the way. Most of us are lucky and things turn out just fine. Early on, though, you should probably also keep in mind that while you are busy in the kitchen sterilizing the baby bottles to sparkling perfection, your kid may be crawling in the living room eating the dirt out of your favorite potted plant. *Mamma mia*, it happens. And still they survive and manage to thrive. Frankly, children are our living proof that miracles happen in the world every single day.

32

Life can be utterly ridiculous. Laughing is key.

Laughter is a gift from the gods. It's free, healthy, non-fattening, soul-sustaining and all-around fabulous. Think of the last time you walked into a restaurant and saw a couple or a group of friends really laughing with all their hearts. Didn't it make you want to walk over to their table, sit down, and join them, uninvited?

We as a society take ourselves way too seriously, and we don't laugh nearly enough. Much has been written about the health benefits of laughter. It's been said to reduce stress, bring greater happiness, and increase immunity from disease. And who couldn't use less stress, more happiness, and increased immunity in their lives? It is said that children laugh about four hundred times a day, while adults laugh an average of only fifteen times a day. Laughter is also known to be infectious, which is why most sitcoms have a laugh track to help induce an audience's laughter. In fact, laughter is so contagious that it can even reach epidemic proportions. I read once that in 1962 in Zanzibar, now known as Tanzania, a few schoolgirls began laughing uncontrollably. Their laughter soon spread to people in neighboring communities. Schools were closed to keep others from catching the laugh bug. The "epidemic" then apparently subsided after six months. I wonder what good would have come if the schools had been kept open during the epidemic!

Laughter also acts as a wonderful distraction, taking the focus away from negative emotions such as anger, guilt and stress in a far more beneficial way than other distractions can do. It also serves to alter our perspective about the gravity of a particular situation, changing the event from one that threatens us to one that simply challenges us. We are far better-equipped to deal effectively with challenges, which kick-start and employ our internal strengths, than we are to deal with threats, which tend to engage our fight or flight mechanisms—neither of which can usually resolve a sticky situation fully or immediately.

I have a good friend who is a world-class laugher. And her life hasn't always been very funny. She's a highly skilled investigator who works in international corporate cyber-security. She is sought-after in her field, and highly regarded. She also had a horrific and obscenely expensive divorce, a long-term relationship thereafter which very suddenly imploded, and three kids, one with a learning disability which kept her busier than it often seemed humanly possible. Through it all, her one constant was laughter, and tons of it. During a particularly difficult period, I asked her about her ability to laugh through things that would often bring others to the brink of insanity. She simply said with a quirky smile that "laughter is better, especially when you consider the alternative of bawling my eyes out, or worse. And besides, do I really want to mess up my mascara?!" We both then had a good laugh. I found that remarkable, but knew that she was absolutely right.

My mother, too, was an A-class laugher. For her, laughter was one of the four basic food groups; it was simply necessary for survival. She laughed her way through the sublime, the ridiculous, good luck, hard luck, heartbreak, and even cancer. She once made a traffic cop who pulled her over laugh so hard when he tried several times without success to pronounce her last name that *he* thanked *her*, then sent her on her way, without issuing a ticket. Indeed, one of my last memories of her was of her, lying in her hospital bed shortly before her death, attempting and finally succeeding in making a crotchety old nurse—known to everyone never to smile, much less laugh—crack up and belly laugh. My conservative-looking mother made a silly quip that a particular piece of medical equipment the nurse was carrying to another patient looked like a very large male anatomical appendage. I'm pretty sure that the nurse had a few minutes added to her life by that wholly unaccustomed fit of laughter.

There are a million-and-one challenges we are faced with as we travel through life. Some hard, some really hard, and some that seem at the time absolutely intolerable and insurmountable. And some definitely are. Some we can fix, though many we can't, despite our very best efforts. But we can make choices about how to deal with the challenges which occur in our lives. Try to find humor in your life at every possible turn and you may find that a jovial approach will make you less stressed-out over the bad things which happen and more amenable to receiving the healthful benefits of laughter. The good news is that your body cannot differentiate between fake laughter and that which comes from something you find truly funny. The physical benefits are exactly the same. So here's one place where you should fake it until you make it. So think about something funny to help you get through the current challenge. And if you can't think of anything funny, think about a useless little fact I recently read that claimed that twenty-three percent of all photocopier faults worldwide are caused by people sitting on them, photocopying their butts. That image might make you giggle just a little bit, and that's certainly a pretty good place to start.

33

Winning every argument is impossible.
It's okay to agree to disagree.

This has been one of the hardest lessons for me personally to learn—first because of my personality, and second because of my chosen profession. However, I have found over the years that this is a very important lesson not just for family harmony, but also for personal happiness.

When I was in college, one of my political science professors invited Neil Abercrombie, then a Hawaii state senator, as a guest speaker to the class. Senator Abercrombie, a man who billed himself as an "outsider" to local politics since he originated from the mainland, was and remains wickedly smart and a somewhat controversial though very likable man. No longer an outsider, if indeed he ever truly was, he is currently the governor of the state of Hawaii.

Back in early 1981, during that lecture Senator Abercrombie gave us, he sat on top of the professor's desk, swinging his legs back and forth like a kid on a playground bench. Even though he isn't a tall man, it seemed that he wanted to be more connected to us when he spoke. Articulate, witty, and possessing a perpetual twinkle in his eye, he is a gifted speaker. Although I can no longer remember the precise content of his lecture from that day thirty years ago, one thing he said has stuck with me all these years: "To argue with someone is to show that you have enough respect for them to try and change their opinion." This statement is true, as it's pretty easy not to waste our breath on those we either don't care about or don't respect.

However, just like a good box of dark chocolate or a fine bottle of Cabernet, what can often be difficult is to know when it's time to stop trying to win, regardless of how badly you might want to grab the gold. To realize that, despite your best research, analysis and efforts, you are just not going to persuade the other person to see your side of the argument or agree with your position. Continuing to argue your position with that knowledge only serves to alienate the other person, or worse, piss him or her off to the point where he or she simply shuts down altogether. In either event, the other person has stopped listening.

Like many good lawyers, I can argue with the very best of them. From every possible angle—inside out, upside down, right side up, backwards, parallel, perpendicular and often diagonally. And sometimes all at the exact same time. Frankly, I am still wondering why no country has made a bid to deem oral argument an Olympic sport. That said (and age and experience probably have something to do with realizing this), at a certain point you need to step back and acknowledge, especially to yourself, that you have reached an impasse. You are just not going to win that argument. And do you really care if Aunt Tilly's marigolds were eaten by the neighbor's resident raccoon? Is it worth it at a Thanksgiving dinner to alienate forever your third cousin who happens to have a weird affection for raccoons? Probably not, even though you may go to your grave KNOWING that blasted raccoon was responsible for the demise of every single marigold on planet Earth.

It is perhaps even more important to keep this in mind where the stakes are higher than dead marigolds or a relationship with a distant cousin whom you see once a decade and who you strongly suspect has a bolt loose. Say a very close friend is about to make an enormous financial investment with a broker you know isn't very talented. In fact, you are aware of several people who have lost vast sums of money by investing with this person. You tell this to your friend, maybe show him some general financial data about returns from other investment vehicles that you know are solid, point out the differences, and explain in graphic detail what you know and how you know it. Still no dice. Your friend just isn't convinced, isn't buying what you're selling and wants to invest a bucket of his hard-earned money with Mr. I. Will Loseyourfunds. In the past, I would have continued making a passionate plea, long after my friend stopped listening, and probably after he was pissed off at me, the messenger. And this would have been not just because I would have hated to see him lose a wad of money (and I really would have), but because I knew I was right and I wanted him to be right also. That way I won and he won too! But after half-a-century, I know that this really doesn't work. Now, if a friend, colleague or client wants to do something I think is insane, even temporarily, I speak my piece, but then force myself to stop. By agreeing to disagree, I have, in addition to turning my personal temperature down, have noticed that there's a collateral benefit in that the door is left open if the other person decides he or she wants to discuss the issue at hand further at a later time. That person is then also not angry with you, and thus is more apt actually to reflect on what you were trying to tell him or her in the first place. After further reflection, the person may come around to your side, but it will be better because he or she will have reached that conclusion on his or her own.

This is by no means easy to do, but is better for everyone over the long haul. Robert Half once said, "Convincing yourself doesn't win an argument." While this may be true, sometimes the only person you really need to convince is the person staring at you in the mirror. Besides, as the actor George Clooney so succinctly said, "You never really learn much from hearing yourself speak." You won't win every argument, and really, it doesn't matter. Agree instead to disagree, and know that that's okay.

34

If you find yourself flying with a flock of birds, fly the other way. Those in the flock don't always know where they're going either.

As children, we often want to fit in more than we want to breathe. No one wants to be too different. In the sandbox, in the clique, in the scout or the ballet troop. Sidney J. Harris said it succinctly when he wrote that "Man's unique agony as a species consists in his perpetual conflict between the desire to stand out and need to blend in." As we get older, of course, we become less concerned with fitting in, but still there are expectations—of ourselves, our families and our peers—with which we must contend. Even though it is often far easier to swim with the rest of the fish in the proverbial ocean of life, sometimes you need to leave the school in which you have become comfortable in order to find out in which classroom you actually belong.

When I graduated high school, the vast majority of my friends and acquaintances were going straight to college or university. And certainly my mother and grandmother would have much preferred that for me, if for no other reason than to diminish their collective Jewish worry. Although in some peripheral way I wanted to also, I somehow intuitively knew that I would not; I actually could not go directly to college. I wasn't ready and I needed to do something different. Besides, I was really sick of school, and couldn't make the intellectual synapse connection between more studies and the rest of my life. So I took what the Europeans call a "gap year" and spent that year working and traveling the U.S. mainland and Canada. Most of my friends thought I was making a big mistake, and their parents thought I was making an even bigger mistake. The parents were convinced I would get sidetracked and never go to college. They were probably also concerned that whatever ailment I had was contagious and would, to their horror, infect their own offspring.

Despite the broken ankle I endured from that stupid industrial accident at that San Francisco hotel which I described earlier, taking the gap year turned out to be exactly what I needed to do— for so many reasons, not the least of which was my encounter with Melvin Belli's office in San Francisco. That experience probably inched me onto an educational path which ultimately ended with me attending law school. Perhaps more importantly, the gap year gave me the time and opportunity to realize that I did not want a lifetime of working for a low hourly wage or being dependent on tips to make my rent. I also realized during that period that I was given a brain that worked pretty well, and I had to do something with it. These were hugely valuable lessons that no freshman college course could have possibly provided me. That I got to see some beautiful parts of the U.S. and a number of not-so-beautiful places along the way was simply an added plus which served to remind me just how lucky I was. Thus, by the time the year was up, I was really ready to start college. Looking back, I probably had a bit more maturity and more direction than the average college freshman possessed.

I rejoined the flock and was comfortable in it. I had a very positive experience with university life, and I was focused in that I got good grades. I also held a thirty-hour-a-week job, and a full load of course work, and took advantage of a lot of available extracurricular activities. However, I was unfocused in that I had changed my major nearly half-a-dozen times. I may have been the only undergraduate student who caused my kind and patient counselor to want to change her *own* career path. With about a year left before graduation, I still was uncertain about my path and thus not fully committed to the work load I knew would be waiting if I attended law school or any other professional graduate school right away. This was made even more complicated by the fact that I had applied to and gotten into two of my top three choices for law school. Learning from experience when a bit wobbly, I once again decided to leave the flock and take another gap year. But this one would be a bit trickier. I had to get my first choice school to agree to a deferment, which I had been told was not always granted, and certainly not a slam-dunk. I had to make a pitch and hope the person reading it thought both I and the reasons for the deferment were worthy to commit a space to me for the following year. If the request was denied I would have to go through the entire lengthy, expensive and time-consuming process all over again, with no special dispensations. I also had to decide if being two years older than my peers at graduation would have a negative impact in relation to potential employers. These weren't major issues in the grand scheme of things, but still required my focus. I needed to buy some time, although at this juncture too, the vast majority of my friends who were going to graduate school were not taking a break, and tried to convince me to go straight through, again concerned that I would get waylaid somewhere. Ultimately I got the deferment from my top-choice school. I then decided that if an employer didn't want me because I was twenty-six instead of twenty-four, that was so absurd that I wouldn't want to work for them anyway. So I commenced my plan for the gap year to end all gap years: a big trip around the world.

I was only two months into the gap-year big trip when I received the crushing news about my mother's terminal illness, which, of course, abruptly changed the course of so many things in my life. In hindsight, the decision to take the gap year was actually a godsend, though not for the initial reasons. Because of how things ultimately transpired—which could never in a million years have been foreseen at the time—the gap year provided me with the time to do exactly what I needed to do with my mother and spend as much time with her as possible. It also had the collateral benefit of firmly putting to rest any lingering notions I had about attending medical school, since, despite my interest in public health, there was absolutely no chance I was going to spend my working life anywhere near a hospital. And more oddly still, had I not taken the gap year and instead been in law school as a first-year student when my mother fell terminally ill, no doubt I would have either flunked out completely or had to quit altogether and restart a year later. Incredibly odd how things transpire, especially when you aren't able to drive the bus you find yourself on.

As things turned out, I was pretty weary by the time I did get to my first year of law school on the east coast. And it showed. For the first few months, I was overwhelmed and out-of-focus. I was also very far from home, and trying to deal with my first real winter. I had left the flock after university in search of certainty about my path. While the gap year may not have provided me with that, it did, however, provide me with a certainty of what I did *not want* for a career path. And sometimes being certain about what you don't want is just as important, as it may provide a clearer avenue to traverse so that you can ultimately learn what it is that you do want. No one in the flock, even your own flock, can possibly know your path, or the journey you should or will take. They may not even be really sure of their own. So if you are not sure if the road you are on is the right one, feel free to pull over, take out a map, and look for directions and maybe even a solitary sign or two. You may end up in a completely different place than you thought. Or in precisely the same one. What matters is that you will have gone there on your terms, taking your own path to get there. And your path is the one you should be on. Regardless of where the flock is headed.

35

Arrogance is really, truly ugly.
You should avoid it like Camus' plague.

In 1869, in *The Innocents Abroad,* one of the world's most famous travelers, Mark Twain, wrote:

> The gentle reader will never, never know what a consummate ass he can become until he goes abroad. I speak now, of course, in the supposition that the gentle reader has not been abroad, and therefore is not already a consummate ass. If the case be otherwise, I beg his pardon and extend to him the cordial hand of fellowship and call him brother. I shall always delight to meet an ass after my own heart when I have finished my travels.

As a veteran traveler, I long ago ceased to be amazed at how some people behave while not on their home turf. This is true of Americans abroad or foreigners traveling in the U.S., but admittedly I am more offended by the former because of the fear that I will somehow be lumped together with those possessing my nationality. Several years ago I was in Europe for an extended period and took a week trip to Sardinia with a friend. While on the beach, I had run out of sunscreen, and left my friend on the sand in search of some. I found a small market a few blocks away, and went inside. While waiting in line to pay, I saw a woman who appeared to be in her mid-forties talking very loudly in American English to the young cashier, as if she were both deaf and mute. The cashier was neither;

she simply didn't speak English. The young cashier continued softly trying to explain her predicament in Italian while the American got louder and louder and more visibly agitated. This went on for about five minutes until I could stand it no longer.

I speak only maybe thirty words in Italian, and most of those have to do with coffee, pizza and ice cream, but it turned out the young cashier also spoke French. The problem was that the cashier couldn't break the American woman's hundred-euro note, and the small market didn't take credit cards, she told me. When I explained this to the American, she got even more irate, complaining about Italy's inefficiency, their lack of English, the fast drivers—and on and on she ranted about items irrelevant to her attempted purchase. I suggested she go to the bank across the street to get change and then come back and make her purchase. Without a word she left the store in a huff. I took this opportunity to apologize profusely for this quintessential ugly tourist's rude behavior and then quickly left before she could ask me from where I came.

"Arrogance and snobbery live in adjoining rooms and use a common currency." Morley Safer once said. And he was absolutely right. It may be tough to break a hundred-euro note in a tiny shop in a small town in southern Europe when you don't speak the language. It is even tougher still when you don't use common sense and human decency to realize and appreciate that you are on *their* turf and must abide by *their* customs and *their* rules. If you want and expect everything to be as it is at home, then you should probably stay home. Why would one expect all Italians to speak English? Does any nineteen-year-old cashier in a small town in Oklahoma speak Italian? In any event, had this American woman just been a little patient and tried to figure out the problem without making a big scene and leaving a bad taste in everyone's mouth in her wake, she probably would have had a good laugh and wished she'd taken a course in basic Italian instead of yelling loudly in English—as if that helps—and coming across as a loudmouthed buffoon.

But you don't need to go global to bear witness to undeniable arrogance. Usually it's sufficient to turn on the television and listen to political hot air or its corollary, teenagers or young adults who are categorically certain they know absolutely everything about all things under the sun, when in fact it is clear they still possess remnants of lingering diaper rash. As you get older, you tend to have less patience for the arrogant among us, and at the same time develop a much keener appreciation of how little you know and how little one can learn in the few years we inhabit the planet.

Arrogance is usually a camouflage for insecurity. Once you become sensitive to that, you are more easily able to identify it and to deflect its impact. And as you get older and grasp more fully how little you know, this becomes easier to do. After all, just because ketchup was sold in the 1830s as medicine doesn't make ketchup part of a modern-day first aid kit. Unlike self-assurance, which results from one knowing one's own strengths and limitations, arrogance, sadly, has virtually no limits. Arrogant people do not see weaknesses in themselves, and indeed are often quite pleased to find and point out defects in others. As we all know, imperfections are inherent in being a member of the human race, so the arrogant among us have clay feet, however well concealed they may at first blush be. Arrogance in all of its forms is a pill, except that some good usually comes from most pills. I can't really think of a single situation where exuding arrogance is beneficial unless of course you are a used car salesman puffing hard to make a sale. Albert Camus said, "The need to be right is the sign of a vulgar mind." Just as the inhabitants of the Algerian city of Oran wanted to avoid the infected rats in Camus' *The Plague*, but couldn't always do so; you will be substantially happier if you make every effort to avoid the arrogant among us. If you can't avoid them, then perhaps by understanding them better you'll at least be able to lessen their impact on your life. You may also want to think about leasing a new car instead of buying that late-model used one you've had your eye on.

36

Things that drive you nuts usually are nuts.
You are not a squirrel.

In Western society today, it seems that there are about a hundred million things that can drive you nuts. In fact, the list is so long that a separate book on the subject probably wouldn't do it justice. Eve probably asserted to Adam pretty much the same thing when she first realized that there was no running water in that lovely garden which they called home.

There are days when it appears to you that, despite the best planning and organization, things go awry and then some. Like the times when the dog has puked up what seems like a week's worth of dinners all over your newly installed carpet, your son left the lights on in his car and is now stuck in a parking lot thirty miles from home, your daughter inadvertently left her lacrosse stick in the garage and the team bus is about to leave for a tournament across town, your husband's meeting ran late and he just missed the last flight to return home, the washing machine has imploded, depositing an avalanche of soap on the part of the carpet not covered in barfed-up kibble, and a client is repeatedly calling to rehash a problem that was resolved a month earlier. On a day like that, hopping on an Airbus bound for Borneo begins to sound very inviting. But despite the intense desire to escape to Borneo, or anywhere other than exactly where you happen to be, sometimes you simply can't. Especially since you no longer have any credit cards, since your wallet got stolen the night before when you left it in your briefcase in the car because your hands were full of a week's worth of overstuffed grocery bags.

So how do you keep from losing your marbles when these things happen, and happen all at once?

The pivotal question to ask, after you step back and take about a hundred deep breaths, is very simple: Will this really matter a year from now? In the vast majority of cases, especially where the temporary insanity is caused by what I call detail driven mania, your answer will, in all likelihood, be no. In due course, you will call the carpet cleaner, your son will call the automobile club and then sit and wait, and your daughter will have to play in the tournament with a borrowed, perhaps lesser-quality lacrosse stick. And both of them will learn important life lessons about personal responsibility and consequences, with the collateral benefit of you not having had to lift a finger in teaching that particular lesson. Eventually, the old Maytag man will finally show up, or you'll get a long-needed new washing machine. Your husband will stay the night in a small town where, too bad for him, the best restaurant is a Denny's, and you may decide that the tiresome client should be referred to someone else, quite possibly a good therapist. Then you'll call the bank and cancel all your credit cards.

Of course, not all problems are of the detail-driven variety. What about when the problem is a very serious one—say, a partner's infidelity or a relative's impending bankruptcy—and thus the answer to the question is a resounding, "Yes, it will very much matter a year from now." This kind of problem may in fact temporarily make you crazy and give you the urge to head immediately to the nearest airport—or, alternatively, make you want to perform major surgery on someone without anesthesia. But you, of course, need to dig a whole lot deeper and decide on a course of action and long-term solution—if one exists, given the problem—that works best for you and everyone else concerned.

Fortunately, though, the vast majority of problems that we face daily and which run the risk of causing you to want to commune with the orangutans of Borneo are not of the catastrophic variety. While you may indeed really enjoy hanging out with primates in the Pacific one day, you might want to save that experience for a time when you can plan it and can really enjoy it, and not just use it as an immediate antidote to the dastardly details of a busy life. And remember, while you may really like nuts, and you may even really like squirrels, you don't necessarily want to be either. Besides, squirrels have a tendency to get fried to a crisp when traversing all those electrical high wires.

37

Thinking and worrying endlessly about the elusive future often results in an inability to enjoy the present. While you are here, strive daily to stay here!

A few weeks ago, I read somewhere "If you are depressed, you are living in the past, if you are anxious you are living in the future, and if you feel content, you are living in the present." That's pretty simplistic, to be sure, but if you stop actually to think about it, that concept makes perfectly good sense. Aimlessly dwelling in the past is usually a one-way ticket to the urban center of Frustrationville. At the same time, tomorrow's grounds can often be too uncertain for concrete plans. Staying in the present is vitally important, but it is no easy task.

In his best-selling book *The Power of Now*, originally published in 1997, Eckhardt Tolle's intensely personal message ultimately reached and influenced millions of readers. Tolle's basic message is that our mode of consciousness can be altered, thereby permitting us to become deeply conscious of the present moment, "The Now," instead of remaining a prisoner of the sense of self our egos provide. Tolle borrowed concepts from several Eastern religions, and while the book may not have given black-and-white practical methods for staying in The Now, it certainly gets the internal conversation going and does require one to think about consciousness and being present in the present.

Sometimes being present is as simple an act as throwing your hands up, or, to paraphrase Tolle, surrendering so you can accept a situation internally without any reservation. This surrender is not to be equated with resignation, but with an acceptance of how things are at the moment. In other words, it's a willingness to yield to, rather than to oppose, the ebb and flow of life.

When my daughter was just a few weeks old, a dear friend and her husband who were then in their late sixties came to our house for dinner. After admiring the baby, who promptly fell asleep as if on cue, my friend walked into the kitchen and asked me how I was doing. I recall reporting that I was feeling fine, though of course completely sleep deprived, and that I was happily nearly back to my pre-pregnancy weight. I did, however, mention to her that I had this continuous, odd feeling in the pit of my stomach. No pain or discomfort, just kind of an inexplicable heaviness. She started to laugh and said,

> Dearie, welcome to the Moms' Club. You will have this feeling in earnest for the next several years, and then it will gradually dissipate over the years, then it will crescendo again when they hit puberty and then it will again subside, but it will never really go away. It simply comes with the territory in the messy land of Momdom. But if you succumb to this angst— and don't you dare—you will miss out on all the amazing things that happen in the process, basically an abundance of everyday miracles that happen, like when you successfully change your son's diapers without getting peed on. Or when they first use the toilet and the litany of other miracles that happen in the first twenty years. Stop planning, and for God sake's stop worrying. The worry will cause you to miss out on all the fun.

And this was coming from a Jewish grandmother no less! Those ladies are the veritable expert inventors of worry. But she had a very good point. It was as if a light bulb went off in my head. In her infinitely maternal, pre *Power-of-Now* wisdom, she was advocating precisely Tolle's best-selling concepts.

In other words, worrying about the future in effect robs you blind of what is happening today. Make no mistake: this is not just a theoretical concept, but an active, conscious practice. Indeed, I constantly have to remind myself to stay present. This is often even more difficult for me because my professional training is based upon what I call angst labor: foreseeing problems and pitfalls and taking concrete actions to avoid them. Angst and worry are kissing cousins; to be sure, they are the Bonnie and Clyde thieves of the present, but with neither their romance nor their chemistry.

I am not suggesting that you live so much in the present that you don't make any plans, don't have appropriate insurance, don't save money for the future or otherwise live with reckless or irresponsible abandon. Personally, I like nothing more than a good plan—especially if the plan involves an airplane or a five-course meal in a good restaurant! It is, of course, a delicate balance, and sometimes it may even feel like walking a tightrope while simultaneously juggling numerous bowling pins overhead. But life does imitate art, and sometimes the circus is as good a place as any to stay focused on the present. Rest assured that you will be in very good company under the proverbial big top, since I guarantee you that a real live tightrope walker is thinking ONLY of the present. Thanks, Barnum.

38

Your problems are perhaps not your most prized possessions. They are, however, still far preferable to other people's problems.

After a few busy months, a friend of mine and I were sitting at a neighborhood deli on a recent Saturday and playing catch-up over the requisite lox and bagels. As a family therapist with a busy practice, she is always able to corner the market with stories of the crazy myriad of problems people either manage to have or somehow get themselves into. Whatever the problems *du jour* are that she might be recounting, it does without a doubt always make for an interesting meal.

During the lunch, my friend was telling me about one of her patients, whom she labeled "Ms. Way Too Much." The moniker stuck because, as she described it, this patient simply had way too much. Too much of everything. Too much money—so she never knew who her real friends were. Too many kids—she had had trouble getting pregnant the traditional way, went to a fertility clinic, and then had triplets. Too big a house—so much trouble. Too expensive a car—so she wasn't comfortable giving her car to valet attendants to park. Too many charity dinners— too boring. Too much sex with her husband. Really? At a certain point in the "whine" session, my friend finally could listen no more and told Ms. Way Too Much, "While I understand your perceptions of these issues, you need to understand that what you really have here are 'quality problems'." My friend said that the look on Ms. Way Too Much's face was a combination of flabbergast and shame, akin to being told that your zipper is wide open while you are addressing the Supreme Court with a full gallery.

While I don't wish to diminish Ms. Way Too Much's perceived suffering, and while I can (tongue-in-cheek) think of half-a-dozen people who would like to trade places with her—at least in terms of the too much money and sex part—the simple fact remains that if given a choice, most of us mere mortals would almost always choose our *own* problems over those of others. Something like better the garbage you know, than the garbage you don't. It is not so much a matter of our familiarity or comfort in the knowledge of our own problems because of proximity, time and experience, but rather our propensity, ultimately, to deal with and accept our own problems. In essence, good, bad or indifferent, our problems seem to become a part of our perception of ourselves.

Years ago when I was living in Tokyo, I became good friends with another American woman who had lived there for several years with her American husband. One evening she called me hysterically and asked if she could come over. An hour later she arrived, and over a bottle of wine told me that her husband of six years had told her earlier that evening that he was leaving her—for another man. Now THAT'S a problem. Never having been confronted with that particular scenario, I did the most responsible thing possible. I opened up another bottle of wine.

My friend ultimately recovered, and went on to have a happy long-term relationship with another man which continues strong today. Years later, when we were sitting in a restaurant in San Francisco, I was telling her about an acquaintance who was in Tokyo at the same time we were. My acquaintance's husband had left her and their two children for a much-younger law firm receptionist who had a ten-year-old child. We later learned during the ensuing divorce that the receptionist's child in fact belonged to my acquaintance's husband. That story, my friend said, was "totally outrageous and would be an absolutely intolerable situation."

I had to think about that for a while. For me, both situations were incredibly difficult to imagine enduring—nearly impossible, in fact. And while I briefly played in my mind the Russian roulette of various awful problems that I thought I could endure, I realized that, thankfully, I needed to go no farther even with empty chambers. However, my friend's reaction to the sad story of my acquaintance was very interesting. If Gallup took a poll, I'm not sure which of those scenarios would be considered worse than the other on the Richter scale of awfulness. The point is that, as terrible as my friend's story was—and it took her a very long time to come to grips with that and move on—she made it clear that she far and away preferred her set of problems to those of my acquaintance. So while I am not advocating embracing your problems as long-lost friends or a winning lottery ticket, I am suggesting that somehow we are, each one of us, capable of handling the problems which beset us either through happenstance or simply bum luck. And it may be that, ultimately, the ability to come to grips with and handle those problems successfully gives us the requisite preference necessary for the acceptance of them. In the end, it may well be best to embrace what's on your personal plate. You may not possess a lust for lamb's liver and leeks, but it may well go over a whole lot better than goat's gizzards and garlic.

39

Make certain your personal glass remains half-full. Even after you have drunk every last drop from it, the water has spilled all over your feet, or the glass has broken into a million kaleidoscopic pieces.

The mind is like a personal garden. If you let a raccoon into it, you'll have a hard time getting it out, since raccoons really like gardens. In the same vein, negativity is like a raccoon that gets in your garden and wreaks havoc with everything in it.

I learned from my mother pretty early on that maintaining a sense of optimism during periods of adversity, or *especially* during periods of adversity, while tough to do, not only helps you get through those difficult times, but actually makes those difficult times easier to handle. About a month after my mother passed away, I brought a few gifts to some of the hospital nurses who had cared for her during those final weeks. In some of the stories they had recounted, I learned, not surprisingly, that my mother had attempted to ease the suffering of other patients in the cancer ward. This was done either by her making her usual litany of ridiculous jokes, often centering on the lousy state of hospital food, or by her attempts to instill hope in others even when, seemingly, there was none. This optimism, I know, was not born from a sense of denial; she clearly knew the extent of her disease, and understood with distinct scientific precision her prognosis. However, given that dismal state of affairs, she was going to be "hogtied in hell or high water" before she allowed that miserable disease to steal the joy of what little time she had left.

This full-glass philosophy applies across the board, and is equally important in application to the day-to-day stressors in life. When situations arise which you must deal with but can't stand—say, doing your taxes or dealing with a difficult person or problem—if your glass is consistently half-empty during that process, it only makes things that much worse. The negative approach not only clouds your vision of whatever you are going through or attempting to address, thereby making it more difficult and seemingly time-consuming, but it also feeds that voracious raccoon in the garden like a smorgasbord on serious steroids.

There's a colleague in my circle whom I've known for more than twenty years. He's smart, good-looking and financially very successful. He is also incredibly self-absorbed and often negative to the point of nausea. When he was in his forties, and going through a very bad divorce following a fairly short marriage, the negativity was to be expected. Somehow, however, he was never able thereafter to view life and what transpired in it with any degree of even partial full-ness of glass, regardless of the relationships he later had, his professional successes, how much money he made or the freedom that brought. Nor did he outwardly express any correlation between his approach to life and his continuing loneliness. Even twenty years later, when I listened to him over lunch recount a story of another colleague, then in his sixties, who had recently found love following the lengthy and devastating terminal illness of his first wife, his negativity seeped through the meal. While he outwardly stated that he was glad for his friend, his jealousy of the man's current situation was patent. It was almost as if his friend's happiness brought home his own unhappiness with his long-standing solitude. It was sad for me to bear witness to that mainly because he saw zero connection between his own attitude and behavior and his situation of two-plus decades. As a result, over the previous several years, many of the people in his circle who had regularly invited him for holidays or dinners with nearly religious fervor, so that he wouldn't be alone, quietly stopped including him in those social gatherings. It was never discussed, but intuitively I understood it. At a certain point, it just became too taxing. The overweight raccoon in the garden wrought havoc with other people's optimism and, simply put, became too depressing to encounter. Whatever bright spots such a person can sometimes bring to the proverbial table are ultimately overshadowed by the psychic collective cost of having them around. It's more than a light drizzle on an occasional outing; that's understandable and normal. It becomes not just constant rain on the parade of life, but a knowledge that no matter what good comes a person's way, it will always be viewed with the clouded vision of that increasingly obese raccoon in the garden. It's a thundering rainstorm that just doesn't let up, even when the clouds start to break and the sun tries to shine through.

It's true that some people are simply more optimistic than others as part of their basic personality traits. Certainly my mother was one of those people. But I know many others as well. For other people, it is an acquired skill, necessary for them to best negotiate the often bumpy and winding road of life. Raccoons are supposed to be pretty smart animals, and while I don't doubt that, they need to be steered clear of in the garden of your life. No matter how bad things can get—and sometimes they can get truly terrible—nothing good will come of communing with a ravenous raccoon who is never, ever satiated. So pick up a glass of water, offer none to any nearby raccoons, take a sip to quench your thirst, then notice that, indeed, your glass is still half-full.

40

Sometimes people who have been close to you get left behind. This may be an unintentional evolution in your life.

As you traverse the globe, whether literally or figuratively, you encounter a myriad of people along the way. Some for a moment, others for a lifetime. And many pass through just for a specific period in your life though their impact may be truly significant despite the relative brevity of the time shared.

Part and parcel of the journey is understanding when it's time to let go of certain relationships. Not because the person has been mean to you or acted in ways which didn't feel comfortable, but sometimes simply because you've grown apart through no one's fault. It is just an evolution in which one person has taken a different path and the other has either decided to stay put or take another path altogether.

I have a wonderful and dear friend in Paris whom I've known for more than twenty years. She's now in her early fifties, with a satisfying career, a nice husband, a beautiful home in the suburbs, and two delightful children in high school. We had lunch recently, and although she was her usual upbeat and positive self, I could tell something was amiss. After the usual details of catch-up were played out, I looked at her intently and said, "Okay, spill." It was then she told me that, while on the outside all was well, she and her husband hadn't had relations in five years. She said she'd tried to get her husband to go to couple's counseling, but he had refused, telling her he "wasn't crazy." So she went alone, which she said had helped her deal with the plethora of feelings she was experiencing. I asked what her plans were, and her usually sunny face turned sad and she simply said, "I'm taking one day at a time, but I will probably leave him when the children finish high school."

This is not an uncommon story, to be sure, but I felt deeply my friend's pain, though could offer little other than a sympathetic ear. This was a monumentally difficult choice, made more complicated, of course, because of her desire to give their children a stable life for their remaining years at home.

As I thought about her situation over the next few days, I kept hearing the one line she said by way of explanation: "We've just grown so completely apart that we have literally nothing at all to say to one another." It stuck with me because I remembered them as a young couple talking incessantly, and laughing, it seemed, all the time. It was difficult for me to reconcile that with her current situation and his apparent unwillingness to attempt to correct the impasse they now faced.

To be sure, we all have in our backgrounds stories such as this one to varying degrees, in which one person grows in one direction, and the other stays put or goes in an altogether different direction. This is, of course, what makes long-term relationships often such a challenge. And of course there is no one-size-fits-all answer in such a situation. There is only the right answer for the affected individuals, or at least the best possible answer given the situation and the various moving parts.

Whatever decision my friend makes, she'll have my unwavering support, as I know her course will have been well-thought-out. That said, whatever path she chooses, there will be difficulties, as neither path is without sacrifice, compromise, adjustment and, ultimately a need for acceptance.

As we travel onward on our personal journeys, we often for one reason or another, have to let go of individuals who had an intense impact on our lives. Sometimes there is apprehension and regret in the departure, and sometimes there is relief and freshly inspired hope and optimism. And sometimes it is a mélange of all those sentiments. Regardless of the path chosen or the eventual outcome, the key is to learn from the mistakes no doubt made along the way, and accept the good and the positive of what transpired and take those with you as you continue your evolving journey onward.

41

Your health is your greatest possession. Guard it fiercely; your life depends on it.

Take care of yourself. We hear this phrase so often, it almost doesn't register anymore. Good health is everyone's major source of wealth. All the money in the world won't put off the Grim Reaper if bad genes or destructive lifestyle are present. It is true that, with a lot of money, you will have access to better healthcare, regardless of where in the world you live. But even so, as we saw recently with the early passing of the genius who was Steve Jobs, all the money in the free world won't change the eventual outcome if your health is truly lost. And without good health, happiness is virtually impossible.

With the forty-two thousand things that can go wrong with children—even before they exit the utero—it's still a miracle to me that they can get to adulthood with all of their limbs attached and all body parts present and functioning. This country has some of the best medical minds and technology in the world, but still medicine and healthcare decisions must be questioned and understood. This is especially the case when a family member is ill or hospitalized. There is much that can go wrong in hospital-based settings, and a neutral advocate on one's side is a patient's best defense against the litany of potential disasters. And certainly, one should question what goes on in a doctor's office as well. That said, I firmly believe in vaccines, and although I have tried to understand the anecdotal evidence behind the decisions of parents who opt out of vaccinating their children, I admit that I cannot. This is especially so given the

213

known benefits of herd immunity, which history has shown to be true: that the larger the percentage of people who are resistant to a particular contagious disease, the smaller the likelihood that a vulnerable person will come into contact with an infected source. I confess to having been more than a bit relieved when one of my daughter's friends, with five siblings and parents who didn't believe in vaccinations, moved across the country.

I have been incredibly blessed with very good health—that strange sound you hear is me knocking very loudly on my wooden desk. Indeed, the only time I've even stayed overnight in the hospital as a patient, other than for childbirth, was for nasal surgery. Three times, in fact. None of the surgeries worked, and I've long ago given up. I cannot breathe at all through the blasted thing. As well, I can go for months at a time and have zero sense of smell. A perfume counter, a French bakery, picking up messy dog droppings—all have the same impact, which is absolutely nothing. Then suddenly, for a few fleeting moments a couple of times a year, I get an extremely hyperactive sense of smell. During those times, the act of merely walking *by* a department store cosmetic counter causes me nearly to pass out from an olfactory overload. Indeed, I may have been the only woman ever living in France *not* to douse myself daily in perfume. And, frankly, under modern interpretations of the Napoleonic Code, that alone may be deemed a treasonous act. I won't even start on the allergies. But truthfully, it is only a malfunctioning/non-functioning, basically irrelevant nose, and I've learned long ago to live with it. In the interim, I have noticed, however, that it is an extremely useful protruding appendage for the purpose of holding up my very cool sunglasses. Who knew there was any other use? In the scheme of things, of course, it is merely an annoying irrelevance, given the magnitude of real challenges that others face. With all that could go wrong by my age, and earlier, a bum nose is just my own personal, clogged-up joke.

So eat your Wheaties, get enough sleep, have your annual physical exam and the "fifty-and-over tests," and above all, count daily your many blessings. And remember that while your health is your greatest possession in the world and should be guarded like the Hope diamond, you also need to enjoy yourself, since no one ever gets out of this world alive anyway.

42

Hope for the best. Prepare for the worst.

If I had a dollar for every time my mother used this phrase, I could have safely retired many moons ago to a lovely chateau in the South of France. My mother was in no way a religious woman, but if she had a spiritual mantra to live by, this was certainly it.

In fact, this concept nearly became for her a way of life, or rather a way of dealing with the uncertainties of life. Above all else, my mother possessed a true abundance of hope. And often in circumstances in which an otherwise-normal person would have long before given up and simply surrendered.

Her overflowing reservoir of hope, however, did not in any way stop her from being conversant with the flip-side of the hope coin: preparation for Armageddon. These laborious "plans" she sometimes made were often hilarious—until of course you needed the fruits of that labor. No doubt these plans were in large part a reaction to being a single parent in a foreign land in the late 1960s long before that was common or fashionable.

Like many uniquely American stories, this one has at its center an automobile. The first car we had following my parents' divorce was a light-blue, two-door Toyota Corolla, which we had when everyone else was driving station wagons similar in size to a typical New York City apartment, only larger. My mother was proud of this little car's petroleum efficiency, and felt very avant-garde in owning it. The fact that she could park it without a small army of onlookers assisting, or without demolishing other fenders, was just an added bonus. Pride of ownership in the blue metal people-mover continued until a young woman sped through an intersection against a light, totally demolishing the little car and sending my mother and her best friend to the local emergency room with severe injuries that plagued both women for the rest of their lives. I was in the back seat without a seat belt, of course, as was common then, and, miraculously, didn't suffer even a scratch.

In keeping with our preparation for the worst, our next car was a dark-blue Chevrolet Chevelle. Not quite a Sherman tank, but three times the size of the obliterated Toyota. There was always a plethora of survival kit items in the car—a thermos or two of coffee or water, fruit, raisins and other snacks, Kleenex, spare batteries, a transistor radio, blankets, and a whole host of other items quite useful in a severe snow storm in the mid-west, but pretty comical on a balmy Pacific island. When I pelted her with questions about why our car always seemed as though we were on the verge of heading to Siberia via the Silk Route, she responded the same way: "You never know what's coming down the pike, and you must be prepared." It always seemed to me like absurd overkill. But looking back, those were the prehistoric days long before the advent of cell phones. So when we once got a flat tire near a deserted cane road and we were stranded for more than two hours since, as it turned out, our spare tire was also kaput, I for one was pretty happy to have the snacks and water with us. When we returned home that evening, I didn't say a word when my mother began replenishing "supplies" in the Chevy, which she had by then affectionately named "Ole Bessie."

Several years later, when I was in college, I made a trip during the Christmas break with a friend whose family lived in Atlanta. His mother generously offered me her very old but trustworthy Oldsmobile to make the ninety-minute drive to Macon to visit my eighty-three-year-old grandmother. I drove to Macon and spent a wonderful day with her, catching up. Around five p.m., I told her I should hit the road to get back to Atlanta.

She really tried to get me to spend the night, as she'd heard a freak snowstorm was headed for the 75 highway toward Atlanta. She even attempted the normally tried-and-true bribe that she would make her famous chocolate cake if I stayed over, all to no avail. In my youthful impatience to get back to my friends, and incredulous disbelief that any snow would actually come to the Deep South, much less a storm, I kissed the amazing old lady on the cheek and bid her adieu. About twenty minutes north of Macon, while on the four-lane highway, the freak storm suddenly hit, and hit with a vengeance I will never forget. It was a very scary experience, as I had up to that point never driven in snow, and it soon became apparent that neither had anyone else in central Georgia. There was zero car control, and the highway became a massive skid fest. My only luck at that moment was that the Oldsmobile was enormous. Then, a few miles north, the skidding simply skidded to a complete halt. It was then that the old trustworthy Oldsmobile heater decided it had provided enough service in its rusty lifetime, and unceremoniously croaked. I was stuck in that freezing car with no blanket and nothing to eat or drink for nearly eight hours until the storm passed and emergency vehicles could clear the road. But what I really wanted all those hours was a rest room, so sure I was that my kidneys would explode! Fortunately, my youthful kidneys prevailed though I still laugh when I think about what my mother would have said of planning for *that* kind of emergency. I'm absolutely certain she had a few ideas up her sleeve.

My mother's life-long philosophy and my very distinct nephrological memories of that freak Georgia storm stuck with me over the years. I now have my own version of Ole Bessie, a twelve-year-old silver Nissan truck fully stocked for a potential Armageddon, of course made far more convenient with portable GPS, cell phone recharger, bottled water of several varieties, power bars, trail mix, Kleenex, beach towels, blankets and the like. My daughter used to say, "Mom, we could live in this car for a month if we had to." I sure hope we never have to even for a single night, but if either hell or high water comes and we do, then you can rest assured, we'll be fed, watered, charged and warm. In other words, we will hope for the best, but should the worst come, we will certainly be well prepared. Though I'm still working on that vehicular bathroom thing.

43

Despite what you want, or perhaps in spite of it, the only guarantee in life is that things will always change. This may seem bad, but is often very good.

The first time I went back to Paris after my beloved friend Sophie died, I spent much of the plane ride over the pond wondering how I would feel there without her. There were so many resonant memories of that city made richer, fuller and more colorful by her presence that I couldn't imagine my beloved City of Lights in her absence. It was as if so much of what was great about Paris for me was inextricably intertwined with Sophie.

Of course there were some bittersweet moments, especially when walking by *Les Deux Magots*, one of Sophie's favorite watering holes on the Left Bank. If I had a Euro for every hour we spent there over the years talking and laughing and people-watching, I would be a very rich woman. I walked by *Les Deux Magots* one afternoon and got about a half-a-block down the boulevard when I turned around and walked back to the café. I decided to have a glass of wine and toast my Sophie. About ten minutes after I sat down outside at a small table Sophie and I had several times shared, which faced the famous Boulevard Saint Germain, my cell phone rang. It was my former secretary calling from Los Angeles. As I was chatting with her, I saw in the distance a vaguely familiar face through the throngs of pedestrians crossing the busy intersection that evening. As the man got closer to the café, I realized it was an American lawyer I worked with in L.A. for a few years, a very nice guy that I hadn't seen in several years. What was crazier was that he and I had shared for two years the very secretary with whom I was at that moment on the phone. I told my former secretary who had just appeared before my eyes, and called out to my colleague with her remaining on the line. My colleague was as surprised to hear his name called out while on a crowded street in Paris on holiday as I was to see him there. And he simply couldn't believe it when I handed him my phone and he learned who was on the other end, especially since none of us was any longer at the same firm. He and his new wife sat down at my table, and together we toasted French serendipity. It was one of those incredibly bizarre and utterly sweet moments in life, and I couldn't help but wonder if Sophie had a hand in that. That was exactly the kind of thing she would maneuver.

I saw Sophie everywhere on that trip. It often made me sad, but more often than not, I was reminded of the many blessings she had had brought into my world. The most important was that she made me a better person by simply allowing me to bear witness to how she lived her life. On my most recent trip to Paris, a few weeks ago, I had dinner with an old friend who had also known Sophie well and who had driven with me to her funeral nearly ten years earlier. He recounted to me that the several years up to the period when Sophie died had been for him *la belle epoch*, the beautiful period. He didn't mean this in a morbid or depressed way because his life was of course good now, but a certain magic and brightness in his life was gone without her. I pondered that for a few days, and the more I did, the more I understood what he was trying to convey to me. It was as if certain periods in your life are so defined by the richness that certain people bring to it, that when they are gone some of that color is likewise diminished, even after the initial sadness and grief over the loss have been resolved. Death, of course, is a natural part of the cycle of life, and while the sweet memories of departed loved ones can often be called upon for sustenance when needed or triggered by an event, some of the color and vibrancy in one's own life is reduced or extinguished altogether by their departure and permanent absence. And sometimes, no matter how badly you want that particular color to come back, it won't. You may have other colors, rich, deep and vibrant, but not precisely the same one. I realized that the best way to honor Sophie's life and the many lessons she imparted was to embrace the many changes that life threw my way and do everything possible to infuse as much color as possible into my life. To that end, every time I am in Paris I stop by *Les Deux Magots* and raise a glass to the veritable rainbow that was Sophie and remind myself that for every sad ending there is at least the possibility of a new and happy beginning.

While it's true that not all change is good, it is a fact of life. I believe more than ever that it's what you do with the perceived negative changes that measure your success in navigating the tough times and living as full a life as possible in spite of them. The great thing about change is that bad things, no matter how bad they appear to be, also, in due course, change. That, of course, is the good news.

While we mere mortals will always be saddled with the challenges and difficulties of dealing with and enduring life's sad, bad and sometimes truly lousy events, very often a proverbial window is opened ever so slightly when a door unceremoniously slams shut in our face. And you never know what is waiting for you just through that window. It may well be the start of something very colorful and truly wonderful.

44

Over-prepare for the important things; then, no matter the outcome, you can take pride in the fact that you did your personal best.

Not enough can be said about over-preparing for the important things in life. In today's world, when so many people seem to be operating at half-speed or not at all, it is even more important to be prepared. Putting aside all notions of cream rising to the top—which may in fact happen if you give the task at hand your personal best—it's about knowing in your heart that you did the very best you could.

Sometimes you are rewarded with success, and sometimes you fail. There is a big difference between stepping up to the plate fully prepared to hit as hard as you can, or simply trying half-heartedly to slide into home plate on a wing and a prayer. In the former situation, if the home run isn't ultimately scored, you are virtually freed from the damnation of later regrets. In the latter, those regrets are almost a guarantee.

Perhaps because of my background, I was infused early-on with what I call the "immigrant-child template." For as long as I can remember, this was our golden rule: Study hard, be prepared and do your very best. As long as I did my best, that was all that was asked of me, no matter what the outcome. That was sufficient when I plowed flesh-first into a spoke-exposed chain-link fence (an accident requiring several stitches) on my first solo bike ride *sans* training wheels, buried my parents far too young, and traversed young adulthood virtually alone in a country my parents had sacrificed much to get to and survive in. In the back of my mind, our golden rule became my own guiding principal.

Simply put, regret is devoid of virtue, a bandit of the positive, a robber of experience. In effect, it creates the false premise that you're entitled to a do-over of what was. Revisionist history is by definition a very dangerous proposition which, if one partakes of it, is a one-way detour to a would-have, could-have, should-have, crazy-making merry-go-round. While you are sometimes lucky and blessed enough to get second chances in this lifetime on things which really matter, you never get a do-over of what was. Ever.

The good news is that as long as you try your personal best, regardless of the task at hand, you will firmly close the door on the emotional thief of the proverbial "what ifs" in life. Thus, whether you try your hand at glass-blowing and break a half-dozen vases but don't lose your eyesight, take the medical school admissions test and score miserably the first time but ace it the second time around, or raise children under less-than-perfect circumstances and find that one of them doesn't turn out exactly as you had hoped, then you can take both solace and pride in the fact that you did your best. You can ask nothing more of yourself. Well, you can certainly ask, but there will be no one home to take that phone call. As a wise woman once said, it is not what they call you that matters, it is what you answer to. Your answer is doing your personal best.

No one scores a home run every time at bat, no matter how talented he is. Not Joe DiMaggio, not even Babe Ruth. In looking back over the last fifty years, I've certainly made my fair share of mistakes—probably far more. Do I regret those mistakes? Not a snow ball's chance. No doubt I am where and who I am partly by virtue of many of those errors. It's not that I view those mistakes as badges of honor, but simply that I realized and accepted along the way that, regardless of the circumstances, I did my personal best. This is all that we can and must ask of ourselves, and it has to be enough.

So give the geraniums a try, attempt to get your pilot's license or raise your children even though sometimes you are driven to distraction. Put one foot in front of the other and do your very best. The outcome will be exactly as it is supposed to be.

45

Use the good china, wear your nice clothes and stop saving things. Today is special enough.

I'm a big believer in using the good china, even or especially for no good reason other than because it's a pleasure. Why should I have to wait for guests to come over to enjoy it? Needless to say, I now have a lot of mismatched pieces. And I couldn't care less.

I remember a visit to Tel-Aviv one winter when I was in my cousin's bedroom and she was showing me the spoils of a recent trip to Europe. On one hanger after another she showed me beautiful sweaters, a new coat, several pairs of shoes and a great pair of leather boots—all with the price tags still attached and the shoe boxes neatly stacked in the closet. This was the case even though she'd been back in Israel over a month. When I asked her why her closet looked like a Macy's window display, she reacted with mock horror and explained that she was "waiting for a special occasion." As she had a demanding job, a husband, three kids and two dogs, I told her that if she were going to wait for a special occasion to wear all of those things, they would certainly be out of fashion by the time she removed the tags. And often that was, in fact, the case. On her last trip to the Israeli equivalent of Goodwill, she had a car full of bags containing brand-new, but out-of-style items with the tags still on them. When I pointed this out to her, she said, tongue-in-cheek, "Well, at least the recipients will get to wear new things." A year later I met her in New York City for a long weekend. But this time, instead of shopping and then lovingly folding and packing her new things up in her suitcase for closet display, now she tore off the tags and tossed out the boxes. And it seemed that weekend that she wore everything that she had bought. Good!

I'm all for special occasions; indeed I love them. In fact, I love them so much that I strongly believe that good champagne ought to be on the Surgeon General's pyramid as one of the four basic food groups necessary for robust health. But squirreling away things for a day that may never come makes no sense to me. Why put off until tomorrow what you can enjoy today? Especially if it is both non-fattening and legal?

My husband reminded me of this a couple of weeks ago. It was a Friday evening after a particularly long week, and he opened up a good bottle of wine to kick off the weekend. Then he walked into the pantry and took out what I knew was our last container of our beloved (legal though very fattening) *foie gras*. Before he could open it, I rather excitedly said, "Don't, it's the last one; we should save it for a special—" and before I could finish my sentence, he leaned over, kissed me like a man on a mission, smiled, and reminded me that "today was special enough." The lonely container of *foie* was then devoured in very short order.

Fortunately for gastronomy's sake, I was heading back to France in a week, so I could replenish our dwindled supply. In fact, heading to the little store where I buy our *foie gras* was one of my first stops after I arrived, lest I return to the States without it. *Quelle horreur!* On that brisk, sunny morning, still a bit foggy from the long flight over the pond, I asked the proprietor for twenty-four containers of our favorite delicacy. He immediately asked if I was having a "*grand fête,*" a big party to mark a special occasion. I smiled at my favorite grocer and simply said, "*Non monsieur, aujourd'hui, c'est assez spécial*"—no sir, today is special enough. He chuckled and winked and bid me *au revoir.* He knew, of course, I'd be back. And probably sooner rather than later.

So use the good china, burn the pretty candles and, for goodness sake, take the tags off your nice clothes, put them on, and enjoy. Today is indeed quite special enough. Especially whenever there is *foie gras* involved.

46

In facing life's challenges, strive to be the driver and not the passenger in the car of your life.

One cannot navigate the myriad of highways and byways of life without encountering a cornucopia of challenges. Some are mere blips on the radar screen of your life; others can bring you to your knees. And sometimes, despite your very best and most heroic efforts, the result you seek will not be achieved. Indeed, sometimes you will fail, and fail miserably, perhaps through no fault of your own.

Nearly fifteen years ago, I was involved in a particularly nasty litigation. Perhaps I should rephrase that, as much litigation has the potential for nastiness, whether because of the subject matter, the litigants, the counsel or the judge. But this matter was the worst I'd ever seen, then or since. Worse yet, this litigation lasted for over four years. It was seemingly without end; sixteen long seasons of pathological Purgatory.

As the matter wound, or rather crawled, through the system, there were three changes of attorney on the other side and four changes of the presiding judge. Finally, we were saddled with a judge who, although then in his sixties was untalented at best, and, perhaps more damning still, a racist and blatantly shameless bigot. Both sides had used their one peremptory challenge to excuse two prior bench officers assigned in the matter for various reasons, and the third judge was, for some reason, quickly transferred to another division at a different court house. So we were stuck with the fourth judge, who made clear from the outset that this was one of his last cases to hear as he would soon be retiring to a more lucrative "rent-a-judge" consulting position.

On and on the case went, with no relief in sight. The judge simply would not decide the various issues, punting at every turn. Then, at several points in the litigation when he could punt no further, he would order the parties to hire extremely costly and unnecessary experts to provide even costlier and more unnecessary lengthy reports with conclusions that the judge would then completely ignore. It was the darkest black hole I had ever encountered, both as a lawyer and as a human being and I often thought the case would do me in both professionally and personally. By this time, the parties had spent nearly half-a-million dollars in attorneys' fees, experts fees, court costs and other costs, and everyone involved was nearly apoplectic, but still there was no end in sight. It was, in a word, hell.

At this point in the litigation, I had a very strong sense that one of the attorneys on the other side had engaged in highly unethical conduct which had severely prejudiced my client's case and which, if I could prove it true, would saddle this attorney with major professional sanctions. However, when I attempted to bring this up, the judge either refused to understand or actively chose to ignore the gravity of the committed acts. It became evident to me that no matter what I did or said, this sorry excuse for a judge simply would neither hear me nor issue a ruling. Being in that courtroom day after day with no resolution in sight often felt like a never-ending meeting to discuss contemporary fools, which of course seemed like an endless discussion. In a last ditch effort to prove this issue regarding the opposing attorney, I filed a motion for the production of certain documents that I knew the other side legally would have to produce. It was a long shot and an expensive one, but it was also the last shot. Opposing counsel filed a motion to quash my request and argued the motion with such force and such venom that it stunned even the semi-comatose judge. It also further convinced me that I was coming close to finding their Achilles' heel. By a miracle for which I'm still today grateful, the judge granted my request, not, I believe, because he thought I was right, which I later proved I was, but because he knew if he denied my motion, that decision would be overturned on appeal.

After three months of a litany of absurd dilatory excuses, at five in the afternoon on New Year's Eve I finally received four bankers' boxes with several hundred pounds of documents literally thrown chaotically inside. It appeared as though a certified public accountant had simply barfed in those boxes and left it at that. By three in the morning, I'd gone through the first three boxes, and though I had organized the documents into a semblance of order, I still had not found what I had hoped to find and what my client needed. I was nearly manic with fear that either I had made a tactical error or, more likely, the other side had illegally withheld the papers I desperately needed. Either way, I feared my client was sunk, as I knew this judge would not for a second entertain a further inquiry, even if an appeal would be forthcoming. With a heavy heart, I plowed into the fourth and final box. Half-way through, there was still nothing of import. I had all but given up, but as I was close to the bottom of that final box, I continued, bleary eyed, exhausted and disgusted. As the sun started to come up on the horizon of a new year, like a phoenix rising from the ashes, I came upon THE SMOKING GUN. The document which proved definitively what I had been arguing all along was stuck backwards and upside down to another innocuous and irrelevant document. To be sure I wasn't hallucinating from exhaustion, I reread the document three times. To paraphrase the gifted Paolo Coelho in *The Alchemist*, it felt as though the universe were conspiring finally to help me escape this endless morass. What I found was so egregious, so outrageous, so incredible, that not only could I not believe my eyes, I simply didn't trust them. I immediately called another lawyer who was familiar with the case, though not directly involved. After I assured him that my house was not engulfed in flames—why else would any sane person call at six in the morning on New Year's Day?—he listened intently, then said what then sounded to me like three of the most beautiful words in the English language: "It's all over." He said he'd shower, make a pot of coffee and call me back in fifteen minutes to strategize. I, on the other hand, went directly to the refrigerator and immediately opened up a bottle of champagne.

As soon as the courts opened after the holiday, I filed a motion to disqualify the opposing counsel. They vehemently opposed it with a fervor of counsel replete with the knowledge that if my motion succeeded, they were going to be ordered out of the case, sanctioned on the record, and perhaps worse for them, forced to walk away from unpaid attorneys' fees that had by then surpassed a quarter of a million dollars. The judge, who had been the very bane of my existence for the past four years, finally made a decision in keeping with the evidence. Not because it was right or just, but because his hands were tied and there was no way for him to manipulate the produced evidence in order to rule any other way. Much to my relief, the matter was settled shortly thereafter. But as is often the case in litigation, especially protracted litigation, no one was really happy; too much time had passed, too much money had been expended and too much emotional energy had been exhausted.

To say that this case affected me profoundly would be an understatement. Besides the time and energy, the less-than-perfect outcome and the toll on me personally, it forever altered what was, up until then, a sacred and holy trust I had held tight in the fairness of our legal system. It was an extremely bitter pill to swallow. All of that said, and despite this experience, given what I know about other legal systems, I still believe that warts and all, our system is better than most, though certainly not for the faint of heart.

What I was ultimately left with after the initial sadness was an understanding that I was not, as a mere mortal, and despite my very best efforts, able to be the driver of this particular car, but forced to be a passenger in a vehicle that was veering off-course toward a mountainous cliff with an empty abyss in plain view. The car eventually righted itself, but by then much damage had been done. I also understood that it was critically important not to get beaten down and give up though admittedly I came perilously close. Being an auditor in that situation simply wasn't an option. I had to show up, stand tall and press on as I was being pummeled by clearly unethical lawyers and a bigoted, biased judge who simply didn't give a damn about what was right or just or the oath he had sworn to uphold.

A few years later, a colleague asked me about this experience. Trying to summarize it would have been impossible, nor did I much want to. Some things just need to go away. In trying to extricate myself from the conversation, all I could think of was a comment that Clifford Wharton, former American ambassador to France, once made: "Listen, I can stand it if a man pees on my foot, but by God, when he tries to tell me it's raining, that's too much." Personally, I have always really hated the rain.

Embracing the lesson of a past negative experience does, in fact, loosen the debilitating stranglehold of its lasting impact. So while you can't always chauffer the vehicle in which you may find yourself traveling for a period of time, that too shall pass. During that ride in the passenger seat though, show up, take several deep breaths, notice the view from the window (however dark and dreary), stand tall, and press onward. If you continue on that path, then eventually you will move your way back to the driver's side. And it will ultimately be a good ride.

47

Find something that makes you feel wonderful and do it every day. Even if only for fifteen minutes.

The best part of this concept is that it really doesn't matter what it is that makes you feel wonderful—assuming it's not too fattening, obscenely expensive or illegal. For some it's meditation; for others it's yoga or walking the dogs. While all of those are great, my daily ritual is coffee. Not just the actual drinking of it, but the entire Gestalt of coffee and what it represents.

From the moment my eyes open, I'm as focused as a homing pigeon, except my goal is the act of making and drinking coffee. From turning the espresso machine on, to measuring and grinding the fragrant beans, to frothing the milk for my first cup of the day—for me it is a near-religious experience, and every second of it is savored with a reverence normally befitting a private audience with the Dalai Lama.

My husband, in an infinitely generous act of kindness, retrieves the morning paper every day, saving for me the front page while he disappears to his gym in the garage with the sports section. Then, for those next fifteen minutes, regardless of the news of the day, all is completely right with the world. It is, for me, my daily fifteen minutes of bliss, regardless of the fact that I must rise at five in the morning to partake in those fifteen minutes. It is, to be sure, one of the highlights of my day.

Perhaps because my mother was born in Israel and my father in Austria, coffee had always played a unique and somewhat revered role in my life. I don't have a single memory of either of them in our home without a cup in hand. Whether the moment was happy, sad, or somewhere in between, coffee was ever-present. It was a stabilizing force during the otherwise-tumultuous 1960s 'way out West. As neither of my parents drank alcohol, simply because neither cared for it, all social life with those who came to our home was focused around the coffee pot, and the conversation which flowed seemingly effortlessly and endlessly with it. It was not the tongue-twisting half-decaf, double-shot, extra-hot, no-foam, non-fat cappuccinos of today. It was from a seemingly simpler time, and was no more than a large pot of fairly watery, hot brown liquid around which all social discourse took place. The coffee's country of origin was unknown, since the corner market's wares had no discernable provenance, delivery big-rigs notwithstanding. Not to have sufficient cream in one's home when my parents' friends came to call (no milk there), as well as real sugar cubes (the pink, yellow and blue stuff had not yet made it to mainstream America despite tendencies to bulging waist lines) was akin to social suicide.

I cannot personally recall my first cup, though that may be because I was less than ten pounds at the time and it was heavily camouflaged in breast milk. Drinking a full cup of coffee at the table, with real cream and sugar, was a rite of passage into young adulthood, probably not unlike today's young adults' first glass of wine or draft beer.

In college, the horrible stuff they served in the cafeteria was more of an instrument that helped one stay awake during a boring professor's class. In graduate school, the course work got harder, and the coffee, thankfully, got better. By then, coffee had also graduated to a more exalted level; not having any coffee on your way to class or not getting enough, was practically academic/intellectual hara-kiri. During those years, coffee was not so much a social event, as something more medicinal in both method and application.

As the years went on, and I traversed the globe for both work and pleasure, coffee assumed an even higher status. The cafés of Europe held their allure as the epicenter of all social discourse and endeavors. They were, and remain, the very extension of one's living room. Young lovers gaze into their rich espressos, workers discuss the union issues of the day over café crèmes, and older folks contemplate their pensions whilst their cups emptied effortlessly. This is by both design, as each city neighborhood has "its" café, and by necessity, as most people's flats are simply too small or inconvenient to accommodate their social circles.

In Tokyo and Seoul in the 1980s, European-style cafés sprung up in the toniest neighborhoods, offering seven-dollar cups of liquid heaven for Asian yuppies in training and Western expatriates tiring of tea and seeking solace in the familiar comfort of a good cup of Joe. Sometimes it was just a little reminder of home when one was far away and on unfamiliar turf. And that would often be sufficient to enable one to forge ahead.

In the Middle-East, coffee houses are the social pulse of the region's quite shaky co-existence with its neighbors. But the coffee houses there also often serve as a forum for the exchange of ideas, social and political discourse, and of course the all-important budding love affairs. In Israeli coffee houses (as in buses, offices, and other places where people are gathered), at the stroke of each hour, on the hour, immediate silence prevails as everyone hushes to hear the news broadcast over discreetly installed loudspeakers or multiple transistors. Then, almost as quickly, the chatter resumes immediately, either with a silent yet synergistic sigh of relief with the knowledge as all is still well in the world, or in pandemonium as the uncertainty of the well-being of loved ones is communally contemplated. In Turkey, Morocco, and Egypt, and nearby locales in Arabia, thick, rich coffee with grounds on the bottom (and of course deliciously sweet, blazing-hot, strong mint tea) is often served in coffee houses—generally for men only—combined with the social sharing of the nargila, a sort of communal peace pipe along with which heated and animated discussions of the issues at hand ensue with great ritual.

While in Indonesia again, the virtual homeland of some of the world's mightiest and greatest coffee exports, I was reminded to my chagrin, that the locals drank some of the blandest and most diluted coffee on the globe—and, perhaps more shocking, much of it was instant! In a headache induced-search of some real java on Java, I finally had it explained to me by a local that much of the good stuff—in his precise words, "the brown gold"— was exported. And in Costa Rica, another big exporter of very fine brew, which is one of that economy's major foundational supports, it was nearly the same story. Other than in five-star hotels often devoid of the local cultural compass, I noticed while traveling this wonderful country that the rich, dark, high-octane coffee for which Costa Rica is famous abroad, was sadly absent *in* Costa Rica. Instead, a weak, watered-down coffee served with regular milk and sugar was widely consumed by the locals. The brown gold, however, was present in bulk for purchase at the airport shops for export upon departure.

In my own kitchen the other day, in the corner all of my ritualistic coffee accoutrements call home, I noted with surprise that each item there possessed a major emotional and life-sustaining component. The stainless round flip-top bowl containing luscious, perfectly shaped white sugar cubes was given to me by a dear friend in Paris when I was there last with her, communing over coffee along with our multi-cultured and multi-colored children. The hand-held, battery operated milk frother was given to me by another close friend while I was in Zurich during a trip where we sat for endless hours over tall cappuccinos contemplating the international paths our lives had taken by virtue of motherhood. The stainless British hot pot (perfect for making a single tall drip coffee using ground espresso, or if you must, a cup of tea) was given to me as a housewarming gift by the kindest and most gentle soul in Canada. Somehow she intuitively knew that for me, that item would turn my new house into a home. Then there was the sadly empty package of coffee beans, which had come from an old friend's coffee

236

farm not far from Maui's Haleakala volcano. The gleaming and costly espresso maker was a luxurious gift to myself. Each item serves its purpose for creating the perfect cup of coffee. But perhaps more importantly, each item also brings me back into that familiar fold of the long-ago coffee memories of my youth and the realization that a great cup of coffee, regardless of from where it hails, or how it arrives, is, just like a cherished friend, by far one of life's deepest, richest, and most lasting pleasures.

I've often said that given enough coffee, I could probably rule the world. That may not be at all true, but it often sure seems that way, especially at five in the morning. So find your bliss and do it every single day, even if only for fifteen minutes. It is time very well-spent. The benefactor may be you, but the beneficiaries are everyone. Now, if you'll excuse me, it's time for a cup of coffee.

48

A short bit of time is all you have. Don't waste it.

It is true that when you lose your parents early in life, your personal clock is forever a bit altered in the sense that you are immediately and summarily infused with a somewhat warped sense of time and its passage. Orphans with some memory of their parents have been robbed, to a certain extent, because the sense of invincibility usually possessed by youth is forever lost to them. The flip side of this cognition is often an acute allergy to wasting time, because you are more aware than others not just of time's fleeting nature, but of the speed and totality of its potential loss. As a result, for people like me, it is a constant struggle not only to remain present and in the moment, but also to remember that others don't always possess the same sense of urgency as I do on matters ranging from soup to nuts.

That said, time is something of which we never have enough. And just like the old cliché that youth is wasted on the young, the fact is that the older you get, the faster time flies by. Worse, there isn't a bloody thing you can do about it, other than make darn sure you don't waste it.

I'm not referring to the usual time thieves of the three T's: television, technology and traffic—although those are certainly very real time-stealing culprits. I'm referring to the other thief— the one in your head. The one which makes you waste your precious time because you are focusing on stuff which either doesn't matter or which you can't currently do anything about.

For example, I have a colleague who still travels quite a bit for work. So she is constantly in motion or on a plane. Instead of talking to the cabbie, reading the paper, or simply relaxing and enjoying the view, she is going over in her head, for the thirteenth time, whether she left the coffee pot on, whether she forgot an important memo on a conference room table or whether there was something she was supposed to do but didn't, or did but shouldn't have. One could chalk this up to the garden-variety neurosis of an otherwise successful Type-A person, but it is more than that. It is the commission of grand theft larceny of time.

Whether the coffee pot was left on or the memo remained on the conference room table, once you are airborne, there's simply not much that can be done. I'm not suggesting you abdicate your responsibilities. But sometimes you have to compartmentalize so you don't waste precious time or energy.

My husband is what I call a CACIC, a Class-A Compartmentalizer-in-Chief. I've never seen anyone alive compartmentalize to such a degree and with such success as he does. This is no doubt why he's such a good manager of people, and often of very difficult ones with competing interests. He must have a thousand tiny little boxes in his head which allow him to shift gears constantly and problem-solve with maximum efficiency and minimum waste, spillage or overlap from one box to another. It is something to watch, and may one day become an Olympic sport. If it does, I guarantee that he'll be there to collect a well-deserved gold medal. And as I've met no one who even comes close to his skill in this regard, he'll probably get the silver and bronze medals as well. His ability to compartmentalize so successfully also means that he falls asleep *before* his head hits the pillow—usually in under two seconds flat—and then sleeps like a dead man all night long. Every single night without fail. It's utterly remarkable.

If you did leave the coffee pot on and you're en route to New Zealand, the pot will overheat and likely disintegrate into a million pieces the next time it's touched, long before you reach Auckland. Not too much you can do about that at

30,000 feet. When you do get home, you may have to pick up some broken glass before you go to Starbucks for a cup of Joe, and on the way back you'll have to stop at the store for a new coffee pot. All in all, perhaps it will take an hour. So why would you waste the fourteen-hour flight worrying about all of the potential downsides to having left that pot on? How can that possibly make any sense in the grand scheme of things? To stop worrying about something, distraction is paramount, and often the best way to do this is to engage fully in something else. And that may be as simple as picking up a book and getting lost in it.

Although Jewish mothers seem to have simultaneously made an art form of and cornered the market on the biggest thief of all, worrying, they do not actually have a monopoly on it. Worrying without a corresponding action is just another enormous time thief. If your hands are tied at the moment, for whatever reason, whether because you are airborne, temporarily insane, or simply stuck in traffic, then getting all riled up and increasing your blood pressure only serves to get you all riled up and increase your blood pressure. It does not aid in compartmentalizing to resolution, nor does it make the problem magically go away. All it does is add another problem to your current heap of troubles. Just as no one will ever say on her deathbed that she wishes she'd worked more (unless perhaps she were working to find a cure for cancer or to rid the world of hunger), no one, I can assure you, will ever say that she only wishes she had worried more or that she really should have wasted more time.

I'm not saying every second of every day has to be filled. Sometimes you just need to sit still and not do much of anything. But occupying your brain and your time with wasteful, useless noise, or worrying endlessly when nothing can be done, is a far bigger thief than most of us can afford to entertain.

49

Age with grace. Emphasis on grace.

Aging in our youth-oriented, truly fixated culture is, if we are really lucky, something which is going to happen. For many, it is a time-bomb, tick-tick-ticking away its constant reminder of our mortality. The creaky knees, the middle-of-the-night bathroom runs, the gray hairs which sprout in places where NOTHING should be, let alone a hair follicle of any color, much less a gray one—oh the indignity! For others, it is an unholy betrayal of our physical being. How can this be when, mentally, we still feel like we're twenty-five (but, one hopes, don't often act it)?

I will be the first to admit to the slathering-on of SPF 50 sunscreen and the donning of a wide-brimmed hat (sometimes, like *The Addams Family's* Morticia, I do this even when the moon shines particularly bright), and confess to eating more fruit, vegetables and brown rice than ought to be legal. And I exercise nearly every day.

The reality, of course, is that time marches on, with or without us, so if we are lucky enough to go with it, we might as well get used to the process. And while we're at it, we might as well laugh about it too. Ensuing wrinkles be damned.

A dear friend of my mom once told me, or rather bellowed at me, "Never, I mean ever, throw out a photo of yourself, even if you think you look like Attila the Hun. When you get older, you will appreciate that photo so much and you'll be surprised at how good you looked way back when." Needless to say, I have a lot of photos, especially from my travels—mainly because this woman was so convincing. And she was right. Looking back at some of those photos when I was thirty or even forty, I don't look pubescent, I seem to appear positively infantile. This was brought home to me again a couple of months ago when I found myself in court with a long-time client who is only a few years older than I am. While seated in the gallery waiting for our case to be called, she leaned over to me, and referring to the state's attorney, whispered into my ear, "Do you think he's ever in his life shaved?" It's not that the state's attorney sported a long Amish- or Hassidic-style beard—it just didn't seem like he was out of puberty, much less a licensed lawyer. Oh Christ, I thought, I really am getting old. Our case was called, we won, and I then got into my aging Ole Bessie and drove back to my office lost in middle-aged thought.

A month ago, while in Honolulu, I had dinner with an old college friend—the same one who, in the middle of the night over two decades ago helped me search for my name on the Bar passage list posted outside on the courthouse window. We hadn't seen each other in over twenty years. As is very often the case with true friends, two seconds after we sat down, the years literally melted away and were back in college, though now with husbands, kids, mortgages and mid-life squarely in tow. In honor of our reunion, I brought her a strand of fresh-water pearls from my last trip to Indonesia. She wore it for three days and nights then e-mailed me that "they feel fabulous against my skin—each pearl is so pretty and yet just gently flawed...I love that."

That thought stuck with me for a few days. Part of aging with grace, I realized, is that we are much like those fresh-water pearls, lovely and gently flawed. Accepting the flaws which increase with age only adds to the luster of our personal pearls. Indeed, that luster and the wisdom that goes with it turns into one of the best things of all: grace.

Grab the sunscreen and Morticia's wide-brimmed hat and, applaud the fact that you are one of the lucky ones. You get to bear witness to the creaky knees and the various aches and pains that come with a life well-lived. Hopefully, you will not knock heads with your spouse on your way to the bathroom in the middle of the night. And if you are really, really lucky, you will also dance the night away—creaky knees and all—at your children's weddings with your new-found friend. The one called Grace.

50

Pursuing a dream may often feel like chasing the howling wind. Even when the clouds are dark, and lightening is about to strike, raise your mast and set sail.

I think I must have wanted to write all my life, though certainly my high school teachers and college English professors would probably seriously beg to differ. Looking back, however, everything I did up to the point when I started writing seriously was in preparation for writing, though of course I didn't know it at the time.

In college I wrote articles for the school newspaper, and regularly wrote op-ed pieces to the local newspaper which, miraculously, they published. In law school I did the same thing. And although I tossed around the idea in college of becoming a journalist, it was more of a passing fancy. I never for a minute ever thought about actually *becoming* or *being* a writer. To be a writer, I have learned, there is one hard-and-fast inescapable truth: you must actually write. Not toy with the idea, not think about it, not fantasize about it, and not talk about it. You must sit yourself down and write. This reminds me of an old native Hawaiian admonition: "*Pa'a ka wa ha ho'ohanaka peni*" which means "shut your mouth and use your pencil." It is, in fact, the only way to write.

I have been keeping journals since the middle of high school; in fairness, most of the early stuff was teenaged rambling—highly unpoetic pubescent angst. Things naturally got a bit more interesting as the years went on and I covered more ground, both literally and figuratively. Several years ago I wrote a screen play about the bizarre adoption experience of an old friend which covered two continents, two countries, two kids, two marriages, and two lawyers. I thought it was a truly remarkable story, but I was obviously alone in that regard, as no one else other than a few friends wanted to read it. Then, later on, I wrote a lengthy overview on an obscure legal issue which even fewer people wanted to read. Hitting the big five-oh however, made me turn once again to writing, but this time with more of a sense of purpose. By the time I was about mid-way through writing *Fifty-Fifty*, I had for the first time since writing my old journals, read though all twenty-plus bound volumes of them. Though for the sake of my progeny, I also shredded several of those volumes after reading them, since some experiences simply do not need to be repeated or shared. With anyone. It has certainly been a wild and crazy, remarkable and wonderful ride. One of the most interesting parts of reading those old journals, however belated, was the realization and the appreciation of the experiences I was lucky enough to have, and of the person I had over the years become. I also was able to see the progression of my own voice and my own writing style.

Of course, as a lawyer, I write for a living. Day in and day out, I put pen to paper. Or in reality, now, I tap on a keyboard and hit the print key. Normally, however, this is writing that no one, sometimes not even the paying client, actually wants to read. They certainly may want the deal or the profits which will eventually come from the transaction, but most don't want to read the fine print they pay me to write. And truth be told, I don't blame them. It is cut-and-dried, meat-and-potatoes legal writing. No humor, no wit, no colorful language, and whatever creativity exists is technical in nature. In fairness, I have often read documents from attorneys on the other side of a transaction or from lenders or their counsel that have made me truly want to jump off the roof of the nearest building. It's no small wonder that most modern office buildings have really big picture windows that you can't open. Likewise, I had the same feeling when I had to review my husband's and my estate-planning documents, so incredibly monotonous were its details. Not to mention that it forced one to actually think about the *purpose* of the documents, which, of course is to cope with death and taxes. Hardly the stuff of a great read. Going to the dentist without the benefit of Novocain would have been far more preferable, if I had been given a choice. However, our estate-planning attorney did not give me that option. To actually sit down, though, and write of my experiences and the lessons I learned along the way, with the idea that someone might actually want to read them and might perhaps find them useful—now that's heady stuff.

I am very lucky indeed for so many reasons. One thing that I am particularly grateful for is that I was able at this stage in my life, both personally and professionally, to take the time to write *Fifty-Fifty*. It was the culmination of a long and winding road, coupled with the desire to articulate and make sense of what came before, so that I may best and most fully enjoy the next fifty years.

If you want to write, simply put, you must write. It may be frustrating and it may be slow going. You may often feel that you don't really have anything worthwhile to say. You may get sick of sitting in front of the computer, or you may get writer's cramp. You may forget everything you were once taught about good grammar and punctuation, and you may temporarily completely forget how to spell. You may feel like you are chasing your tail, or perhaps worse, the wind, which, unlike your tail, you can't even see. But if you want to write, then write you must. Whatever your dream is, you must take the first step, and then the next one after that, and then the next one after that. If you want to sing, you must open wide and sing, even if you first start in the shower when no one is home and then progress to a glee club or church choir. If you want to paint, you must pick up a brush and a canvas and start painting, even if you feel compelled to hide your first results in the back corner of a closet. I am not suggesting you quit your day job, starve your kids, empty out your IRA accounts and become a brain surgeon, unless perhaps you already happen to be a physician! But if you can pursue your dream without abdicating your responsibilities to those who depend on you, then you owe it to yourself to try, and to try your damnedest.

As Franklin D. Roosevelt so aptly put it in his 1938 Fireside Chat, "To miss the tide and perhaps the port; I propose to sail ahead. For to reach a port we must sail—sail, not lie at anchor, sail, not drift." So even if you feel sometimes that the clouds are darkening as you embark on the pursuit of your dream, and you think that lightening may strike, raise high your personal mast. Pick up the pen or the brush, start singing, start running, climb the hill or the mountain, or start to pursue whatever it is that is your dream. And set sail. It may not always be smooth sailing, but it will be your boat. You will be the captain, the first mate, the chief purser, the cook and the rest of the crew. Stay the course, and it will be your own personal journey. Just for you, because it's your dream. No passports, shots, visas or money changers needed. Enjoy the ride, wherever it may take you.

Afterword

My first international trip occurred when I was an impressionable twelve years old. My childhood best friend had an uncle living with his wife and children in Guatemala City, Guatemala. In an act of either incredible generosity—or maybe just temporary insanity—my friend's mom, Gita, who also happened to be one of my mother's closest friends, invited me to tag along on a three-week adventure to Central America with my best friend and her brother and sister.

To say that this trip was a watershed event in my life would be a colossal understatement. During this very-exotic-at-the-time adventure, I bore witness to a variety of extremes that left an indelible mark on my developing young consciousness. There were extremes of undeniable poverty, despair and sadness, coupled with extremes of incredible natural beauty, surprising wealth, arrogance, and seeming disregard for those less fortunate. It was a juxtaposition that made a monumental impression on me which remains today, despite the intervening years.

Located in an upscale suburb of Guatemala City, the home we stayed at—a three-story villa really—had massive walled gardens, a large swimming pool, and an ominous-looking man guarding the entry gate. The house also had several staff working there who managed and took care of everything in the house, including the people living in it or visiting those who did. Frankly, those hard-working employees catered to their employer's every possible need or whim. And then some.

At that point in my life, I had never known anyone who employed a housekeeper, much less anyone with an entire household *staff*. Clothes, meals and other necessities (and some things not so necessary) mysteriously appeared, disappeared and reappeared with a speed that was nothing short of miraculous to a twelve-year-old's eyes. Caring for the four of us was, of course, added to the myriad of other duties for which these employees were responsible. I remember these people who worked in and around that compound as gentle and kind, and possessing a remarkable abundance of patience for the four obnoxious foreign pre-teens they often had to look after. This patience was especially necessary since at the time none of us kids yet had any Spanish language skills, except for being able to name the almighty childhood holy grail of *helado de chocolate*, chocolate ice cream. That not one of us kids contracted diabetes that summer remains an unexplained Mayan medical mystery.

Once we stepped outside the high protective walls of the compound, into the *real* Guatemala we went. Just as I had never experienced at that point in life the kind of wealth my friend's family possessed, I had also never seen that kind of abject poverty seemingly at every turn. Gita made certain we saw it all—the good and the beautiful, and the bad and the ugly. She had rented a minivan and hired a driver and together we traversed this beautiful country of consistent contrasts. There was a plethora of painfully thin and unbathed children wearing rags and begging for money in front of highly ornate and cavernous churches replete with eighteen-karat gold statues and other gold decorative items. There were young and hungry-looking children nearly everywhere we turned, selling chewing gum, cigarettes, newspapers or whatever else they could carry or fit onto a small rectangular tray and maneuver in noisy, congested traffic and stifling heat. And of course I will never forget that there were girls, not much older than my best friend and I, who themselves were for sale to whoever had a few quetzals to spare.

There was also the undeniable ethereal physical beauty of Lake Atitlan and its environs and the shockingly vibrant colors of hand hewn textiles and other wares at Chichicastenango.

There was the intoxicating aroma of freshly ground corn tortillas, and pungent chili and other spices that would simultaneously make your nose burn, your eyes well up with tears and with what was left of your voice, plead for water the moment you swallowed. It was a constant existential tug-of-war between awe-inspiring, magnificent new impressions and indelible experiences, and the crushing sadness and despondency of the human condition. Exiting one particularly ornate, gold-encrusted church one afternoon in sweltering heat, the five of us were enveloped by perhaps a dozen extremely poor children who walked with us *en masse* to our minivan, hoping, I imagined, for some spare change. The mustached driver gently ushered the five of us into the van, and, as he pulled away slowly from the curb, Gita, stared out the window and said incredulously, in her accented English, "Can you even try and imagine a country with such resources that prefers starving children *and* solid gold churches?"

Gita was born in Bulgaria, was a holocaust survivor, and, fortunately for her, ended up in Israel right around statehood. Ultimately she settled in the U.S., married, had children and led a very comfortable, colorful and extremely full life and, because of her extensive charity work, was regularly in the company of both high-octane politicos and well-known Hollywood glitterati. As happens in many war-inspired familial stories, Gita and her brother went different directions to restart their lives. He first went to Mexico for a few years following his departure from Israel, and then settled in Guatemala where he married, had children and thrived. Although Gita no longer wanted for anything at all, her background and her travels made it inevitable that she had borne witness to plenty of poverty, and had seen far too much of its twin sister, human suffering. Gita was also such a strikingly gorgeous and elegant woman that she could stop traffic speeding along the autobahn of life—and she often would, if something got in her way or she needed something to be done. She spoke several languages fluently, including (fortunately for the four of us) Spanish. Thus, as her pre-pubescent traveling-companions/ charges, we were lucky enough to experience Guatemala at a time and in such a way that few would have been able to do.

Without a doubt, that first trip abroad changed me completely. It altered how I viewed myself as a human being and forever modified my perception of my place in the world. I would never again be able take my modest but complex beginnings for granted, nor could I, in the clarity of hindsight, ever dismiss their importance to the person I had become. And I would never, ever be insensitive to the hardships of others living in circumstances virtually out of their control. The seeds were also then planted for the development of a lifelong and chronic allergy to those who believed that there was virtue in hunger and poverty, or the ones who sought for whatever reason to exploit them.

On the last Wednesday in May of my fifty-first year, I was in a taxi en route to the airport when I learned that Gita had suddenly passed away during the previous night. As the plane I boarded climbed to cruising altitude, I thought of the irony of learning this news as I embarked on another adventure. Gita had had such an enormous influence on the very genesis of my love for travel—not to mention providing me with a dear friend, her daughter, whom I, blessedly, still have today. As the plane turned eastward, I sat back and took solace in the knowledge that although Gita had started out life during an unimaginably difficult era, she had had a long and prosperous life, lived it well, done exactly what she had wanted to do, raised three terrific, productive children and was able to enjoy her several grandchildren. Along the way, she changed another child's life in a monumental and everlasting way. For that, and much, much more, my gratitude abounds. *Bon voyage, ma cherie, et s'il te plait quand tu arrives au ciel, donne ma mère un gros bisous de ma part.* Have a good trip, my dear, and when you get to heaven, please give my mom a big kiss for me.

JLK

CPSIA information can be obtained at www.ICGtesting.com
Printed in the USA
BVOW010107110912

299943BV00002B/1/P